Pornography and Genocide

Pornography and Genocide

THE WAR AGAINST WOMEN

Thomas Trzyna

CASCADE *Books* • Eugene, Oregon

PORNOGRAPHY AND GENOCIDE
The War against Women

Cascade Books
An Imprint of Wipf and Stock Publishers
199 W. 8th Ave., Suite 3
Eugene, OR 97401

www.wipfandstock.com

PAPERBACK ISBN: 978-1-5326-5997-3
HARDCOVER ISBN: 978-1-5326-5998-0
EBOOK ISBN: 978-1-5326-5999-7

Cataloguing-in-Publication data:

Names: Trzyna, Thomas, author.
Title: Pornography and genocide : the war against women / Thomas Trzyna.
Description: Eugene, OR: Cascade Books, 2019 | Includes bibliographical references.
Identifiers: ISBN 978-1-5326-5997-3 (paperback) | ISBN 978-1-5326-5998-0 (hardcover) | ISBN 978-1-5326-5999-7 (ebook)
Subjects: LCSH: subject | subject | subject | subject
Classification: CALL NUMBER 2019 (print) | CALL NUMBER (ebook)

Manufactured in the U.S.A.   MARCH 7, 2019

A dedication. I don't know who you are, Isabelle. We were talking, a friend and I, in a coffee shop outside Seattle, about what we were working on. When we had finished, you interrupted us and said you had been listening. Your father, you said, was a Bosnian war criminal hiding in Germany. You introduced yourself, and we exchanged some names and addresses. Perhaps you have contacted the helpful experts I suggested. I thought of the students who used exam essays to reveal they had been raped. It's all around us if we open our eyes, the violence, the war against women.

This book is for Margaret and Alex, too, who model strength and egalitarianism. Thanks to my mother, as well, for speaking forcefully about the status of women in our world.

TABLE OF CONTENTS

INTRODUCTION

THE THESIS AND PLAN of this book are straightforward. There is an ongoing global war against women that can be defined as genocide. This book will propose an expanded definition of genocide by calling into question both the content and the logic of the United Nations' definition of genocide and by asserting that ongoing genocidal assaults and preparation for genocide are the condition under which women live.

The word "genocide" is used here in two senses that mask an important point. Genocidal actions against women are ever present, even though that genocide may not always take the form of physical violence against women. Similarly, a state of war includes many forms of pressure, preparation, intimidation, deprivation, and other harms, even though war as active combat and killing may be sporadic or intermittent. Genocide against women is constant because the preparation for assault is so. The genocide against women defined here differs from other terms for the killing of women because it is constant and aimed at all women. The terms "gynecide," "gynocide" and "femicide" have been introduced for important reasons. These words describe a spectrum of murder that sometimes focuses on adult women and sometimes focuses more on the practices of female infanticide. Female genocide will be defined in this book as a pervasive and ever-present system of identifying, targeting, and destroying women.

This continuing state of threat and destruction forces the world's women to live at all times and in all places in stages five to six of Gregory Stanton's eight stages of genocide, where the first stage is awareness of a difference and the final stage is denial that anything happened at all. Many women experience stage seven, genocidal killing itself, and such genocidal killing is a steady, routine, and ongoing phenomenon in some nations (Stanton, "8 Stages of Genocide"). Women are identified, classified, symbolized, dehumanized, objectified, and subjected to organized systems of discrimination and targeting. Groups of men are prepared to take action against women, and women are then subjected to campaigns of murder and other forms of violence that leave them sometimes dead, often profoundly damaged, victims of post-traumatic stress disorder, catatonia, or what has recently been named resignation syndrome (Pressly, "Resignation Syndrome"). For the most part, societies deny that these activities are damaging or even taking place. Genocide of women is routine, as the evidence will show, and pornography contributes to the slaughter. In some cultures, women kill other women themselves as part of longstanding traditions of female infanticide. Moreover, women are trained to participate in their own oppression. To cite a local instance, some of the first-year female students at a university where I taught took part in initiation activities that included "flashing" the metropolis from a hilltop in the center of the city. The message was about sexuality, availability, and being reduced to sexual organs. One can pass over these instances as trivial; however, when one examines the broad sweep of these activities globally, they are not trivial at all.

Stanton's taxonomy of genocide fits the definitions established by both the United Nations and the Rome Statute. The point of this book is to show that once the definition of genocide has been appropriately broadened to include women as one of the groups subject to genocide, in addition to groups defined by nationality, religion, ethnicity, and other stated characteristics, it can then be readily shown that women live under a steady threat of genocide.

This genocide has several motivating factors. One is sexuality itself. Another is a group of cultural traditions in which male children are preferred for economic reasons. Girls get raised and marry into other families, so their economic value is lost, particularly if one expects assistance in old age. Another motive is sexual predation, simply the sexual satisfaction gained from violence itself, because most pornography includes violence in addition to the violent exercise of sexual power implicit in forcing individuals to be filmed or presented pornographically. These are only a handful of the many factors that produce genocide. Therefore, the overarching thesis of this book is that when women are killed, those killings follow from well-established customs that have lasted as long as we have history, and therefore there is no violence against women that is not in some way a direct consequence of a millennia-old system of war and genocide. That may seem a large claim. But a review of the mind-numbing evidence of violence against women makes the claim at least plausible and probably fully convincing.

My aim is to turn upside-down a common view of the killing of women and outbreaks of genocide. Much of the progress that has been accomplished on these issues, since Ralph Lemkin's first definition of genocide after World War II and Catharine MacKinnon's work to establish rape as a form of genocide in her work before the International Criminal Court— most specifically in the Akayesu case—has focused on genocide as an aspect of armed conflict or war, however those may be defined. The point of this book is to make a case that genocide—specifically genocide aimed at female humans—is a constant condition in which the groundwork is always present (Moses). Outbreaks of killing bodies or killing souls (Shengold) may be precipitated by states of war, but they occur routinely under conditions that do not involve armed conflict. The basis of this case is the fact (one not particularly difficult to authenticate) that those early stages of genocide are always present in the lives of women, even in such simple transactions, as MacKinnon has pointed out in an opinion piece in *The Guardian* (December 2017), of women prostituting themselves through sexual gestures when they work as waitresses or in other service roles.

Pornography is the systematic portrayal of woman as objects that can be traded, abused, assaulted, murdered, and monetized. While some argue that pornography is a healthy introduction to normal sexuality, the evidence indicates that a very large majority of pornography portrays violence against women. It is clear that the consumption of pornography is strongly related to domestic violence and to outbreaks of other forms of violence against women, whether carried out by individuals or by groups. Pornography is also an international industry that generates billions of dollars of income and engages in human trafficking of its subjects. Celine Bardet, to cite one example, describes the trafficking of truckloads of women out of Bosnia long after the occupation of the area by international peacekeeping troops. Ankur Shingal and Tracy McVeigh describe the Devadasi temple prostitution system in India and the trafficking associated with that practice. Norah Msuya describes similar systems in several African nations, and the International Peace Institute has carried reports of the trafficking of Ethiopian girls into the Kenyan prostitution market, just to cite a few examples (Gastrow, International Peace Institute). The International Justice Project published a recent piece on the broad problem of sex trafficking in Africa and Asia (Berrios). Closer to this author's home,

MyNorthwest.com in April 2017 reported that local police estimate that about five hundred teenage girls are trafficked for sex in Seattle at any given time, some as young as twelve years old. The title of the article tells the sobering truth: "Child Sex Trafficking—as easy in Seattle as ordering a pizza."

Making the case for this two-part thesis means pushing the boundaries of some familiar definitions of war and genocide, though this book is far from the first to make that effort. When the total number of women killed by murder, infanticide, bride murder, and other causes during the twentieth century far exceeds the total number of people (male and female) killed in traditional wars, purges, civil wars, and mass starvations, then it is fair to ask by what definition that killing of women, for as long as we have human history, does not constitute both an ongoing war and a process of continuous genocide (Qiu; Downes; Pinker; Sen; Bongaarts and Guilmoto; Liisanantti and Beese). When one gender is selected for systematic slaughter, that constitutes a form of genocide, even though killing women as a group was not included in Raphael Lemkin's initial definition of genocide in the 1940s or in subsequent definitions adopted by various international authorities, including the United Nations. It is not hard to show that women live everywhere in conditions of separation, symbolic identification, and dehumanization, with many organized social systems in place to deny them equal rights and opportunities, and in some cases to kill them selectively. That women are not always murdered *en masse* by armed gangs of men does not make the huge toll of dead women any less a genocide.

The final point of this book is to show the way that the enormous global pornography industry, joined by many small global cottage industries and the widespread consumption of pornography, works to aid in the objectification and dehumanization of women that make female genocide possible and easier to carry out. When South Africa suffered from an epidemic of rape and murder, it was then that Hugh Hefner's three multinational pornography companies lobbied to increase their presence on the South African airwaves, working to introduce 24/7/365 televised pornography in a nation already awash in print pornography. Hefner's companies made these efforts at a time when members of the South African national judiciary pointed out evidence from trials that rapists and murderers used pornography extensively and took cues from the pornography they consumed, as avowed by Kenneth Meshoe, president of the South African Christian Democratic Party ("La Justice Sud Africaine"). Pornography has also become a different kind of industry, not merely the slick products filmed in the United States and other centers of professional pornography, but also the sometimes impromptu and sometimes carefully planned and widespread filming of pornographic torture of male and female victims of campaigns of ethnic cleansing, community genocide, and political oppression. Sometimes these films are made with professional video equipment, and sometimes they are filmed on iPhones with the threat that the materials will be made available on the web to humiliate and psychologically destroy victims of gang rapes, sodomies with sharp objects, and other forms of sexual abuse and torture (Allegra, "Le Viol"; Allegra, "Subjugate Men"). Sometimes the materials are uploaded to the web for the enjoyment of other sadists and people who hate the same ethnic groups. During the Bosnian genocide, such films were aired on the primary Serbian television network (Bardet). Pornographic films and pictures are monetized in one way or another through direct sales or through memberships in websites.

Correlation is not causation. The relationship of pornography to sexual violence is complex. The strong correlation between increases in rape and genocide on the one hand and increases in pornography on the other can be read in many ways. In some cases, people charged with rape point to pornography as a stimulus and/or a source for models for what they have done. However, pornography is a form of violence in itself. When rapists and killers film what they do, the making of pornography is another way of killing or humiliating and destroying victims. Pornography is violence that stimulates more (and is also the visual product of) violence.

This book does not say anything that is not in some way already well known. My objective is to organize the data, to reshape the definitions of two key terms, war and genocide, to show how Stanton's eight stages of genocide can be used to describe the permanent global situation of half the world's human population, and to underscore well-known data about the role of pornography in the dehumanization of women that makes killing facile. The use of pornography to abuse men will be mentioned as it arises, for in some nations rape and the filming of rape and murder include both men and women as victims, and in the case of Libya in recent years there has been a special focus on raping men in order to destroy their sense of self-worth, to cut their contacts with their communities, and to render them impotent in every conceivable way as citizens and persons (Allegra, "Le Viol"; Allegra, "Subjugate Men"). It is also important to establish the ways in which rape and torture constitute forms of genocide, as genocide is now defined following Catharine MacKinnon's success in Akayesu and as the Rome Statute is now interpreted by the International Criminal Court. The limitations of the United Nations' definition of genocide are taken up early in this book. People do not need to be killed to be destroyed, to be paralyzed by post-traumatic stress disorder, to be isolated from their families and communities, and to become victims of what has been called "resignation syndrome," in which survivors of torture and rape are able to do little besides lie in bed in a fetal position.

This book grew out of a previous study, *Cain's Crime: The Proliferation of Weapons and the Targeting of Civilians in Contemporary War.* In reconsidering the data in that book, I was struck by the observation that Gregory Stanton's assessment of the stages of genocide so accurately described the everyday condition of women everywhere. *Cain's Crime* reviews the work of Amartya Sen, a winner of the Nobel Prize in Economics, and others who have estimated the number of missing women in the world and the reasons why so many women are missing in specific nations and cultures. Here I have tried to add some of the other common causes of excess female deaths through intimate murder and such causes as substandard medical care. A fair estimate is that during the course of the twentieth century, over 330 million women were killed for just some of these reasons, a number that approximately equals the current population of the United States of America. Moreover, the killing continues at the same rate. This and other numbers will be repeated several times in the course of this book because the enormity of the situation is hard to grasp.

The discussions and data presented here that trace the effects of pornography are indebted to many international data bases, but above all to the important work and writings of Catharine MacKinnon, Andrea Dworkin, Melinda Tankard Reist, Celine Bardet, and others who have argued for the position that there is no "good pornography," only pornography that objectifies, dehumanizes, and places women in peril, and who have often worked in situations of great danger to bring international attention (and sometimes legal action) to bear on atrocities including mass killing and rape with the production of pornography as part of the destruction.

Pornography and Genocide systematically proceeds to make its case, beginning with what may seem to be a detour: a brief analysis of the Sumerian *Epic of Gilgamesh*, which has been called the earliest work of literature, though perhaps some Indian works predate it. I think it important to emphasize an obvious point: women have been set in an inferior position and subjected to predatory and violent actions from the beginning of written history. The problem of gynecide can be addressed only by challenging the way that humanity conceptualizes the status of women.

The book then takes up the definition of war: Is there a war against women, or are there "official" definitions of war that rule out using this word in reference to killing large numbers of a group that makes up half of the human species? While the international community now defines "armed conflict" rather than "war," many listings of casualties continue to exclude those killed because the conflicts are civil wars or fall short in some way of earlier definitions of war. Next, can the systematic killing of women be called a form of genocide? Gregory Stanton's eight stages of genocide are applied to the ordinary lives of women. If it appears that women are in fact the object of an ongoing genocidal war, then what is the role of pornography in that war and what is the scope of that industry? Finally, what does contemporary history show us about the ways that these forces come together in such atrocities as the filming of women raped in Bosnia and Serbia, the rise of rape and pornography in Central Africa and South Africa, and outbreaks of violence and rape in many other places? The book closes with reflections on what might be done to end the longest of all wars. Throughout, consideration will be given to the problem of deciding what constitutes evidence, because there is a predictable conflict among experts about precisely what it would take to prove that pornography, or all the other common forms of misogyny, causes deaths. On this, as on other aspects of the argument, I am grateful for tips and advice from Catharine MacKinnon and Melinda Tankard Reist.

For the record, this book was written without researching pornography by examining it on screen, though I have drawn on data gathered by specialists who have examined contemporary pornography and interviewed pornographers in the process determining, for example, that 80 percent of porn involves violence of some kind directed against women (Dines, *Pornland*; Castleman, "How Much of Porn"; Gilmore, "Latest Porn Statistics";). Ms. MacKinnon and others, who have pointed out the dangers of pornography and the human trafficking that is a major part of that industry, have often been attacked by those who think there is "good" or normal pornography that is a healthy part of human sexual life. Early in this project, a male friend suggested to me that studying this issue without using porn was like writing a cookbook without trying the recipes. His comment reveals the depth of our social programming. He meant to be funny. (Perhaps my friend would think that writing about the effects of pornography without indulging in pornography would also be like designing and selling weapons without personally killing people with them.) As Ms. Tankard Reist and others have shown, attitudes like this are where the problem begins, with the idea that objectifying and dehumanizing women just a little bit is fine and should even be encouraged as part of normal sexual and personal development. To some extent, researching this book on the web has been difficult because as soon as the terms rape, murder, and porn are put into a search engine in any language, what tends to come up are not news reports, studies, and institutional documents, but rather the websites of pornographic films that offer violent images. Occasionally, my computer screen has been flooded with images of teenage girls in Indonesia, Africa, and other locations, lying on their backs, looking shocked, though their frozen looks include the smiles that their abusers probably demanded. There is debate over how much of the World Wide Web is devoted to pornographic content, though 4 percent has been suggested as a reasonable estimate (Ward, "Web Porn"). Drake Baer's essay on recent Canadian research estimates four billion hours of viewing PornHub, a major site, in 2017 alone (Baer, "There are 3 Kinds"). Those are staggering figures if one considers the scope of the Internet. The cloud is dark. The research here has been limited to English and French, not only because of the author's own limitations, but also because French language sites offer rich resources about Francophone Africa, former French colonies in Africa and Asia, and also more broadly a different perspective on international news. British and other English language sources from outside the United States have been used extensively because of their broader coverage of international news.

I am also indebted to the late Gershon Legman, who is credited with crafting the phrase "Make Love, Not War." Mr. Legman was the writer in residence at the University of California, San Diego, in 1964–65, when the new campus admitted its first freshman class, of which I was a member. I bought and read his once-banned book *Love and Death*, which makes an important point about violence and sexuality. Why, he argued, is it legal to portray so much violence in comics, movies, and television, when it is illegal to portray sex in those media, even though it is legal to engage in sex acts and illegal to commit acts of violence? Legman wrote his book before television treated audiences to full color shootings, autopsies, and the other forms of escalating violence and sexual violence against men, women, children, and babies, levels of violence that are now common. On the other hand, he protested vehemently against pre-Comics Code Authority comic books that portrayed extraordinary violence with strong sexual overtones. Violence in the media arguably does lead to violence in public, though that topic continues to be debated because of the difficulty of determining precise causation, as in the case of most other technical debates about causative factors. What Legman missed is that sexual representations of women, which objectify and dehumanize women, also contribute to violence, even if those representations are not explicitly violent. Again, 80 percent of pornography contains (often extreme) violence against women. That violence is associated with later violent acts. Legman himself was concerned about the amount of violence mixed into presentations of sexuality; however, his own works, such as his collection of sexual limericks, included violent material (Legman, *Limerick*). Most importantly, pornography that does not show violence still objectifies and dehumanizes, making violence easier to commit.

During my first week at college, I walked Black's Beach in La Jolla for the first time. It is still hard to reach, some five miles of fine-grained, pinkish sand at the base of a three-hundred-foot cliff, a place of staggering beauty where at night the waves break blue and green with phosphor. Some other male students had sculpted a figure of a nude woman from the sand. The artistry was impressive, the figure full-sized. One of the young men took a five or six-foot piece of driftwood, a slightly crooked sun-bleached branch about six inches in diameter, and jammed it into the sculpture's vagina. They laughed and left the stick pointing toward the sky. The point—a poor choice of words—seemed not so much to represent intercourse as to represent impalement. What kind of species are we?

The object of this book is simple: to change the conceptual framework for discussions of pornography and genocide. If the arguments presented here are persuasive, then that is good. If my case is not convincing, perhaps the attempt will lead to fresh conversations about the toll of pornography and the ways in which the female half of humanity is systematically and perpetually targeted. Moreover, to make a connection to my last book, *Cain's Crime*, what is "normal," though terrible, about the treatment of women is exacerbated, augmented, and increased by conditions of open warfare or civil war. Many of the accounts and statistics presented here were gathered in war zones, and while there is abundant evidence that women are targeted routinely in times when there is no official or declared armed conflict or war, conditions of open warfare eliminate many normal taboos. For the most part, armies are composed of men who have been separated from their families, forced to go to war, and exposed to actions that numb their normal moral sensitivities, though those same men at home may be among those who commit rapes and other acts of violence within or outside their marriages.

While this book was in process, the case of movie producer Harvey Weinstein hit the news (Vagianos, "Gretchen Carlson on Harvey Weinstein"). Rather than being noted and forgotten, that case of male predation led to a series of disclosures and to radically different public responses to rape and sexual harassment. Michael Fallon, the British Minister of Defense, resigned over stories of his sexual aggression (Stewart and Mason, "Michael Fallon Quits"); Kevin Spacey lost major film contracts, and the director of a new film in which Spacey was the star decided to recast the main role and refilm every scene. The significant and thoughtful television interviewer Charlie Rose was fired from his positions, with many journalism awards subsequently stripped from his record. Progressive American senator Al Franken was forced to resign; Donald Trump, now president of the United States, again faced accusations of sexual predation from over twenty women, though his comments before the election did not prevent him from being elected; the voters of the State of Alabama weighed whether to elect a man accused of pedophilia who argued that the United States would be better off if all the constitutional amendments after the Bill of Rights were repealed. Those other amendments outlawed slavery and granted women the right to vote. Other public figures have been named and shamed; many have been forced to resign positions or end careers. A movement began of women who identified themselves as victims of sexual aggression, using the symbol "#MeToo." Will this movement lead to permanent change? Emine Saner asks in *The Guardian* if this is the end of the patriarchy. Probably not, though it is reasonable to expect some degree of change, and perhaps awareness has been heightened for a time. Some notable progress has been made by what MacKinnon has called butterfly politics (*Butterfly Politics*). Newspapers have begun to run pictures of galleries of notable male politicians and actors who have been plausibly accused of one kind of sexual assault or another.

What this book offers to the discussion is a sober assessment of the larger historical background, the war against women that has flamed for as long as there is any kind of historical record at all. The discussion needs to proceed if for only one single reason: Republican candidate for US Senate from the State of Alabama, Mr. Roy Moore, was accused of molesting several teenage girls. A member of his church who is a spokesperson for the Republican Party, as well as the auditor for the State of Alabama, said in response to the charges against Moore that, after all, Joseph molested Mary, a teenage girl, so there was nothing to condemn (Solis, "Alabama State Rep"; Moran, "Bill Maher"). Whatever one may believe about the Christian religion or any other system of faith, such a defense of pedophilia indicates the extraordinary degree of acceptance of sexual predation and, to use Gregory Stanton's categories, the power of that last stage of genocide, pure denial that anything happened, that anything is wrong with abusing half of the human species.

While this book includes parenthetical documentation and a full bibliography, I will wager that in our emerging world, more readers will turn to their computers than to bibliographies and in-text citations. The reading and writing of books is changing very quickly. Our focus now should be on thinking critically about information rather than on amassing bodies of information. We read now with the Internet at hand so that assertions and data can be readily checked. It follows, then, that an author's responsibility and function are changing. The object of this book is to argue a position and to provide an adequate body of evidence to support that position, not to set forth a comprehensive or global set of references. Moreover, a book like this one can and should be updated by running fresh searches on the web. This book could easily have been far longer, as the topics can be researched readily in even more reports from international agencies, NGOs, governments, and press in many languages. Once one keeps the stages of genocide in mind, news stories daily leap out from the page that fit one or another of the eight categories. The object has been to provide enough citations from a variety of sources to establish the case. Readers are invited to pursue their own lines of inquiry both to confirm and to challenge what is presented here.

The *Epic of Gilgamesh*, the oldest surviving work of human literature, is a good place to begin to understand the historical global normal.

chapter one

PRELIMINARIES

The *Epic of Gilgamesh* Reconsidered

THE *EPIC OF GILGAMESH* is perhaps the oldest surviving work of literature. It may be as many as four thousand years old. S. N. Kramer, in his study of the ancient Sumerians, called Gilgamesh "the hero par excellence of the ancient world" (*Sumerians*, 45). This is high praise. Gilgamesh may have been an actual Sumerian monarch, though his story is full of mythical elements. His friend Enkidu's story is reminiscent of Samson and Delilah: sex with a prostitute tames Enkidu, and so she shears the hair from Enkidu's body (Gerig, "David and Jonathan"). Gilgamesh seeks the tree of immortal life and meets its keepers, Mr. and Mrs. Noah, though the Noah figure goes by the name of Utnapishtim, and the island paradise he and his wife inhabit, like Adam and Eve, contains only a tree of life, rather than trees of both life and moral wisdom.

Gilgamesh is an epic figure indeed in his journey to destroy Humbaba, the monster who protects the cedars of Lebanon. He is still more epic when, following the death of his friend Enkidu, he goes forth on a solitary quest to discover a remedy for death. Those who have studied the history of ancient Dilmun (now Bahrain), the life of Alexander the Great, or the pre-Islamic divinity Al-Khidr will have come across parallel stories of a wonderful garden isle in the Persian Gulf where the tree of life grew. In fact, a Google search will bring up the current tree of life, which manages to grow out of a desert rock on Bahrain. Alexander the Great sent his navy, according to one story, to find that tree of life when he lay dying in what is now Baghdad (Trzyna, *Meeting God*).

Yet the *Epic of Gilgamesh* tells another story as well. Characteristic of much literature, the individual fragments that compose the surviving story set problems that must be solved. Gilgamesh is a hard man on his people. He forces them to build city walls that he allows to lapse into disrepair. He asserts his right to have intercourse with every virgin. The gods respond to the people's complaints by sending down a wild man who is covered in hair, lives among the animals like Tarzan, and poses a threat to Gilgamesh's dominance. Gilgamesh responds to this threat by hiring a prostitute to seduce this man, Enkidu. When Enkidu is weak from sex and shaved of his coat of hair, Gilgamesh defeats him in a fight and the two become fast friends. When the gods allow Enkidu to die for having killed Humbaba, Gilgamesh tries to defeat death and bring his friend back to life. Ultimately, the Noah figure tells Gilgamesh where to find the plant of life, which lies off the shore of his island, though a snake emerges from the sea and steals the plant before Gilgamesh can use it. The story ends fatalistically, true to the ethos of early religions. We are playthings of the gods, who will not tolerate success or competition. Foundation burials in ancient Dilmun consist of the skeletons of snakes with their tails in their mouths, as well as a rounded piece of malachite in each snake's mouth that is meant to represent a green pearl, which is a symbol of eternal life in many pre-Islamic stories.

Look more closely and the structure of this ancient society reveals itself. Shamhat, the prostitute, bears the name "the luscious one." Maybe she is just a luscious one and she has no personal name at all. Perhaps she is a temple prostitute, though that distinction is hardly relevant, as prostituted women are abused, whether living in a temple or a hovel. That is true today of the Devadasi, who are women dedicated to Hindu temples in India. She moistens Enkidu with her vulva before drawing him into her for his first sexual experience. To be pedantic, pornography is literally a description of prostitution. The epic tells us that Shamhat is aroused as well, and thus initiates a basic myth of prostitution: that prostitutes are sexually excited and enjoy their work.

Gilgamesh does not meet Enkidu first, or try to introduce him to an eligible princess. Instead, he tells a local hunter to take a prostitute out into the wild and entrap Enkidu by means of sex. Meanwhile, back at the capital, Gilgamesh spends his evenings down at what is called the "house of the virgins," where he engages in serial rape of all the young women in the nation.

14

Gilgamesh explains that his motive for entrapping Enkidu is to humanize him. A man is humanized or completed by a sexual experience with a woman, though at the same time sex makes a man weak and easier to defeat. Women both complete and defile men in various ways, according to the earliest work of literature.

The earliest work of human literature describes a culture in which a king rules, in which families and fathers are weak, in which all girls are raped, and where some women serve as prostitutes. The earliest work of human literature is in fact a piece of pornography. This same demeaning view of women is so familiar that it does not elicit much comment from the translators and editors, who focus on the more heroic themes of the battle against the monster and the quest for eternal life. How did the power relationship between the sexes reach this nadir, and to what degree, if any, has that relationship changed? One might say that the portrayal of women's status in Gilgamesh is an outlier. If so, one would need to show that women are in significantly better places in Homer, the Bible, or even the works of Dostoyevsky. *The Gospel of Thomas*, one of the documents discovered at Nag Hammadi, has Jesus say that women have no souls.

I leave the question to the reader, noting merely that one scene in Emile Zola's *Germinal* stands out because of its rarity. During the height of a coal miners' strike, the serial rapist who runs the town store and who trades food for sex with the miners' wives and daughters falls off the roof of his building as he tries to escape the mob that has broken into his store to seize food. As he lies dead on the ground, the women cut off his private parts and mount them on a stick that they carry before them as they march, like a banner declaring their liberation. Does this kind of retributive sexual violence occur often? The only instance that comes to my mind, apart from one marital case in the United States, is a news story from the period when Africans rose up and attacked the Arab merchants and rulers of Zanzibar, shortly before Zanzibar joined with Tanganyika to form Tanzania. In that instance, African men paraded the genitals of Arab men they had slain (perhaps as retribution) for the role Zanzibar played in the slave trade. I can offer no citation for this, only an indelible memory from seeing photos and descriptions in the *Los Angeles Times* in the days following the revolution.

Human literature opens with a tale in which "heroic" men oppress, rape, and prostitute women. Does this constitute evidence of a war against women?

What Rights?

First, however, just what rights should women expect? For insight on this question, before examining the war against women, the genocide against women, and the international standards for genocide, the International Declaration of Human Rights deserves to be recalled. Developed under the leadership of Eleanor Roosevelt and passed by the United Nations in Paris in 1948, the Declaration upholds the rights of all genders. As its second article states, the Declaration applies "without distinction of any kind, such as race, color, sex, language, religion, political or other opinion, national or social origin, property, birth, or other status." Seventy years after the passage of this Declaration, the evidence indicates significant shortcomings with respect to the rights of the female half of the human species in the following areas that will be examined in the course of this book:

Article 3: "Everyone has the right to life, liberty and security of person."

Article 4: "No one shall be held in slavery or servitude; slavery and the slave trade shall be prohibited in all their forms."

Article 5: "No one shall be subjected to torture or to cruel, inhuman or degrading treatment or punishment."

Article 6: "Everyone has the right to recognition everywhere as a person before the law."

Article 7: "All are equal before the law and are entitled without any discrimination to equal protection of the law. All are entitled to equal protection against any discrimination in violation of this Declaration and against any incitement to such discrimination."

Article 8: "Everyone has the right to an effective remedy by the competent national tribunals for acts violating the fundamental rights granted him by the constitution or by law" (pronoun usage has changed since 1948, though it continues to be significant that in writing this universal declaration, the male pronoun was used for all persons).

Article 12: "No one shall be subjected to arbitrary interference with his privacy, family, home or correspondence, nor to attacks upon his honour and reputation. Everyone has the right to the protection of the law against such interference or attacks."

Article 16.1: "Men and women of full age, without any limitation due to race, nationality or religion, have the right to marry and to found a family. They are entitled to equal rights as to marriage, during marriage and at its dissolution" (note that full age is a matter of dispute in many nations; in some places, girls are married at very young ages, which affects their ability to exercise any rights they may be granted).

Article 26: "Everyone has the right to education."

Other articles from the International Declaration of Human Rights could have been cited as well, and many of them were and continue to be statements of aspiration rather than statements concerning the actual state of affairs anywhere. The state of women is now and has been one in which very large numbers of women in many parts of the world do not have safety to live; safety from interference; safety from conditions of servitude; safety from abuse, torture, and degrading treatment; or equal rights before national tribunals. Women in all nations at all times are subjected to some of these threats, and the totality of that mistreatment and second-class status amounts to a global war.

What War?

Andrea Dworkin and Catharine MacKinnon have written extensively about the "war against women." Before knowing of their work, I described a war against women in my book *Cain's Crime*, based on a review of the work of Amartya Sen and several others who have calculated the number of women who are missing in the world because of female infanticide, murders of brides, and other cultural customs like female genital mutilation. This work was first published in a groundbreaking article by Sen in 1990. While teaching at an urban university, I was surprised to learn how few of my students, male or female, were aware of this research or any implications it might have for their interest in world affairs. Speaking at adult forums, I have found a similar lack of awareness of this state of affairs. These numbers of missing women, women who have been deliberately killed, do not take into account totals of women raped or murdered in intimate relationships around the world. Dworkin coined the term "gynecide" for this ongoing genocide of women. Others have used the term "femicide," and there is a statute in Guatemala that addresses femicide by name as a special form of murder (Guatemala, "Genocide in Guatemala").

The work of Sen and others began with Sen's analysis of population census figures drawn from governments and other institutions around the world. One can, of course, question the accuracy of those figures. What Sen found compelling was that there were far fewer women than one would expect in many nations, taking into consideration normal death rates and the characteristics of various population age cohorts. Current estimates based on Sen's methodology indicate that about 108 million women are missing at the present time, though Bongaarts's and Guilmoto's estimate for 2035, as noted in my book, is 150 million (see Bongaarts and Guilmoto, "How Many More Missing Women"), and there is a United Nations estimate that puts the number at 163 million in Asia alone for the year 2005 (also see Scaruffi, "Wars and Casualties"). If one assumes that the rate of killing is relatively constant, as the social forces driving female infanticide and other forms of femicide are, it is possible to make an estimate of the total number of women killed in each century. For example, figuring that there are about three generations in a century, and using the global population growth statistics for the twentieth century, with a rise from about two billion people to seven billion, it seems that about 330 million women were killed in the twentieth century because they were female. Of course, the cultural factors involved have probably existed since the time of Gilgamesh, if not earlier, so one is looking at a state of war against the female human population that is as old as our common history.

Totals for the numbers of women murdered annually in intimate relationships and the numbers of women killed in honor killings can be added to this figure. The UN High Commission for Refugees offered the following global statistics for 2003: One third of women are beaten, coerced into sex, or otherwise abused. Two million women are sex-trafficked annually. Ninety million women in Africa suffer from genital mutilation. Sixty million women are missing from sex-selective abortion, infanticide, and neglect.

The Business Human Rights Organization states that fifty girls are sold each month to tourist hotels in Kenya for pornography and sexual trafficking (Amran, "50 Underage Girls"; "United Nations Offices on Drugs and Crime"). A Wikipedia assessment estimates that ninety-three thousand women are murdered each year globally, which would mean well over six million in the coming century, without adjusting for population growth ("Homicide Statistics by Gender"). The UN Population Fund estimates five thousand honor killings each year, a figure supported by other authorities ("Honour Based Violence Awareness Network"). The *Nation* published a report that estimated a rape a minute, as well as a thousand corpses of women killed after rapes each year in the United States ("Rape a Minute"). That works out to eighty-seven thousand rapes per year in the United States alone.

The task of this chapter and the next is to confront problems of definition. The notion of a "war" against women has been questioned, according to MacKinnon and others, because of the way that war has been defined. Currently, the phenomenon of war is called "armed conflict," yet the United Nations' definition of armed conflict still requires at least one of the parties to a war to be a "government of a state." Here is the UCDP Armed Conflict Definition: "An armed conflict is a contested incompatibility that concerns government and/or territory between two parties, of which at least one is the government of a state, results in at least twenty battle-related deaths in one calendar year" (Melander, "UCDP Armed Conflict"). If one wishes to bring a case for a war crime to an international tribunal, there are specific standards for war that must be met. In addition, as I show in *Cain's Crime,* many tabulations of casualties from wars rule out deaths in civil wars or in other forms of combat that do not meet these narrowest and most precise definitions. Similarly, the definition of genocide is limited to a precise set of criteria accepted by international organizations, even though Raphael Lemkin, who coined the term, offered a much broader concept that included wiping out a people by attacking its cultural monuments, for example. Some scholars are now attempting to revise the official definition of genocide to include Lemkin's concern about cultural monuments. (Until recently, this was one focus of a philosophy research project at the Open University.) Under a definition that included major monuments, genocide would include the destruction of the huge Buddha statues in Western Afghanistan by the Taliban, the destruction of classical monuments in Syria by ISIS, and many other recent attacks on mosques and museums in war zones such as Iraq. Such a definition would also include the whole historical record of civilizations wiping away the memories of past inhabitants, such as druids, followers of other early religions, Native Americans, and those early African civilizations that possessed traditions of art and writing. The focus here, however, is on the present, on the fact that the war and the genocide continue, and that there is little reason to think that the numbers of dead are likely to decrease unless something deep in human civilization changes.

Catharine MacKinnon, Celine Bardet, and others have worked for years to build a case for genocide in the Balkans that would meet the standards of the international courts. Their work should be examined by those who are interested in the legal details and capable of understanding the complexities of the international court system. The object here is not to address these issues with the legal erudition and extensive experience that they bring to bear, but rather to make a common sense and *prima facie* case that may move others to action and that may support the work of the legal experts.

During the twentieth century, approximately 250 million people (a quarter of a billion) were killed as a result of wars, civil wars, and other genocidal actions such as the massacres in Cambodia, Stalin's purges, and Mao Tse Tung's Great Leap Forward (Scaruffi, "Wars and Casualties"). This estimate is detailed in my previous book and can be checked on a variety of websites and publications that set different standards for counting the dead, some of which were listed above. As noted already, during that same century, upwards of 330 million women were killed simply because they were women, many of them because they were unwanted female babies or brides. There may be some overlap between the two counts, as it may be that some of the dead in wars, purges, and civil wars include women who were murdered because they were female infants, unwanted brides, or otherwise disposable women. Of course, many of those 250 million were women killed in combat, as civilians, and as victims of genocidal actions motivated by racism and nationalism. It may be that upwards of 450 million women were killed either in war or simply because they were female.

Adding the 250 million war dead to the 330 million murdered women gives a figure of more than half a billion people killed in the twentieth century, which is equivalent to about a quarter of the global population at the turn of the twentieth century. Reciting these numbers does not help to understand them. They are beyond comprehension in the basic sense that one cannot bring the idea into any kind of focus that makes it unified, manageable, or possible to visualize.

The point of relating these staggering numbers of deaths is simple. If the ongoing slaughter of women kills that many people, likely more than all the "official," state-sponsored violence of a century, doesn't the sheer number of dead justify using the word "war" to describe what is going on? Besides, all of these deaths are in fact official and state-sponsored in the sense that they are mandated by national cultural policies that are grounded in traditions, just as are systems of law or commonly understood ideas about civic duty, or any of the other assumptions and common learning that provide foundations for official systems. To put it slightly differently, while official law may be that it is illegal to kill, when there is both a cultural tradition of killing and also a pattern of looking the other way in cases of female infanticide and bride murder, those deaths are officially sanctioned in the same way that pogroms were officially sanctioned in Eastern Europe and that lynching was often tacitly permitted by authorities in the United States. Tacit means silent. To be silent in the face of an evil is to consent to it and to make it a part of the government, even if there are no official laws that sanction those acts. Saying this is no different from saying the following: the United States has the highest rate of imprisonment in the world. People of color are disproportionately imprisoned, as Michelle Alexander's work abundantly demonstrates. The statistical reality is that the United States has a profoundly racist system of justice, even if the laws on the books look color-blind, and even if the Supreme Court declines to admit statistical evidence of racism. Similarly, the statistical and demographic reality is that women are killed at a rate that surpasses deaths in conventional wars.

Another way to look at these numbers is to note that American soldiers in World War II stood about a 1 percent chance of being killed in battle ("United States Military Casualties"). About 38 percent of troops were in supporting, non-combat roles ("U.S. Military World War 2"). Some troops, of course, faced far stiffer odds, including those who flew in bombers over Germany and those who operated machine guns in battles such as Monte Casino. Most of those who served in combat, however, had good chances of returning home. American troops also ran an additional 1 percent chance of being seriously injured. If one examines the total female population of the world and the number killed, then about one out of every thirty-five girls and women is murdered, according to the kind of research done by Sen, the United Nations, and others who have run the numbers on the population statistics and examined the cultural traditions that underlie the killing of women. So, on the face of it, a woman stands about a 3 percent chance of being killed, compared to the 1 percent chance that a World War II GI stood of dying in battle. Obviously, such a crude comparison leaves out much of the context. Still, that crude estimate is a place to start thinking about the level of danger in which women live, always.

That estimate of one out of every thirty-five women leaves out the "ordinary" murders that are harder to identify by looking at broad population statistics across the globe, because the research of Sen and others focused on nations where there are significant traditions of gynecide, including India, China, and some parts of the Arab world. That means the ordinary deaths of women caused by other forms of misogyny may not be as obvious in population data from the rest of the planet. The Youth Advocate

Program International (YAPI) states that female infanticide is practiced in many more nations where the total numbers of deaths may not change the population statistics as radically as they are skewed in China and India ("Discrimination against the Girl Child"). Pakistan's problem is comparable to that in China and India. One site estimates 3.1 million missing women in Pakistan ("Female Infanticide in Pakistan").

In Bangladesh, according to a study by the University of Kent quoted in an article by Taqbir Huda, a Bengali journalist, there are about 2.7 million missing women. She writes about the preference for sons in her country, where a study of 850 families found that 93 percent of those families preferred to have sons. Men depressed because of the birth of daughters sometimes take action against their unwanted children rather late, including two cases reported by Huda. In one case, a father burned his nine-month-old daughter to death; in another a father tossed his two-month-old daughter into a pond to drown. In addition to those killed after birth, there is also an increasing tendency for those who have the resources to abort female fetuses selectively.

Other nations where female infanticide takes place commonly, according to YAPI, are North Korea, Nepal, Algeria, Egypt, Jordan, Libya, Morocco, Syria, Tunisia, Turkey, Cameroon, Liberia, Senegal, and Nigeria ("Discrimination against the Girl Child"). In the case of North Korea, for example, Rachel Denhollander wrote for *LiveAction* concerning a United Nations report that described strong evidence that babies born in prison camps are killed, that women repatriated from China have their babies killed on the assumption that they are part Chinese, that efforts are made to abort fetuses that may be of mixed national origin, and that there is additionally a widespread sterilization of the disabled (Denhollander, "North Korea's Rampant Forced Abortions").

A slightly different picture of female infanticide or selective abortion is given by the first global study of the topic commissioned by the United Nations and published in July of 2016. This report by the Women's UN Report Network on Female Infanticide Country Data listed the following nations as having unusually high numbers of male births or children ("Female Infanticide"). In rank order, these nations were China, Azerbaijan, Armenia, Vietnam, Georgia, Albania, India, Pakistan, Tunisia, Nigeria and Nepal (World Economic Forum, "Global Gender Gap Report"). There is a clear social preference for boys in these nations; in some of them, there was extensive evidence either for ongoing infanticide or for selective abortion.

The report stated that there were nearly ten million sex-selective abortions in China from 2000 to 2014. The most skewed ratio of all was for Liechtenstein, with 126 boys for every 100 girls, a finding based on CIA country study data (Eveleth, "Liechtenstein"). The UN report offers no explanation for this data. Liechtenstein is a predominantly Roman Catholic nation with strong laws against abortion. Women gained the right to vote there in 1984, and have relatively low participation in business, employment, and leadership.

To repeat the level of danger, one out of every thirty-five women killed means that there is about a 3 percent chance that a woman will be killed, or about three times the risk of death to a United States soldier in World War II. In addition, many studies indicate that about one out of every five women suffers sexual assault or rape (Department of Veterans Affairs; Bureau of Justice Statistics, "Rape and Sexual Assault"). That's 20 percent of women who are seriously injured. That would mean that women are twenty times more likely to be injured than American soldiers in World War II. However, to be fairer, perhaps this 20 percent of women damaged by rape should be compared to the number of soldiers who return with Post Traumatic Stress Disorder (Department of Veterans Affairs, "PTSD"). A study published by Medline estimates PTSD rates of 31 percent for Vietnam, 10 percent for the Gulf War, 11 percent for Afghanistan, and 20 percent for the continuing Iraq war ("PTSD: A Growing Epidemic"). So perhaps it is more reasonable to say that the world's female population suffers from psychological trauma at rates similar to those of recent American war veterans. Again, if the effects of the assaults on women are comparable in type and scope to the effects of officially declared wars, is it not appropriate to describe the ongoing state of threat to women as a war? A war, moreover, that is everywhere on the surface of the Earth, not localized to specific places such as Iraq, Syria, or the Congo, where over five million have been killed in recent decades. Many observers describe the Congo as the world's rape capital (Trzyna, *Cain's Crime*).

The US Department of Veterans Affairs maintains a website on sexual assault and PTSD, so the department of the US government that deals with soldiers must view rape and sexual assault as consequences of war. This site states that 94 percent of sexual assault victims experience PTSD in the period immediately following the assault, and 30 percent still experience PTSD nine months later (Department of Veterans Affairs, "PTSD"). Therefore, at a minimum, 6 percent (30 percent of the 20 percent assaulted) of women have both been sexually injured and have persistent PTSD, a number that can perhaps be compared to the 20 percent of those who return from recent combats in the Middle East with PTSD. 6 percent is less than 20 percent, but it is still a large number of human persons. It is critically important not to fall into the trap of thinking that only large percentages matter.

If something produces effects, deaths, and injuries like a war, then it is a war.

To those who would argue that the word "war" should be reserved for official state actions, there are many possible rebuttals. When the United States invaded Afghanistan, some Islamist fighters were declared illegal combatants because they were not fighting for a recognized government. This definition of their status was one reason given for sending captives to Guantanamo and denying them protections of various international treaties. By that same standard of what constitutes a recognized combatant, the American Revolution was an illegal war because it began before there was a widely recognized American state and continued when that state was still not generally recognized by other nations. This game of definitions has been played often with various results, as in such cases as Palestine, Western Morocco, Taiwan, East Timor, and many other circumstances where peoples are denied status as nations and where their conflicts are sometimes considered beneath notice or recognition.

Moreover, it is a fact that the term war has been indiscriminately used to describe national efforts to combat non-state parties when convenient. The United States has declared a war on "terror," though terror is not a recognized state, and the word "terror" in this case stands for any number of vague ideas, including Islamic fighters who use guerilla war tactics and other terrorists with different ideologies. Those on the other side of this war against terror can easily argue that they are the objects of a campaign of terror, because very powerful nations have claimed the right to intervene wherever they wish, with or without the approval of the United Nations Security Council. Members of Pakistani wedding parties, killed because they are misidentified, and civilians accidentally killed in missile strikes against ISIS targets in Syria—to name just two publicized examples—might easily argue (if they were still alive to do so) that they were victims of campaigns of international terror waged by nations so powerful that they are immune from sanctions, even though they may be subjected to international criticism or condemnation.

The United States has also declared a war on drugs and a war on poverty. Apparently, governments can use the word "war" as they wish. The *Atlantic* magazine published an article about the "war on boys," pointing to the high rates at which boys are expelled from school, boys' low achievement on national standardized examinations, and boys' lower rates of college attendance in recent years (Sommers, "War Against Boys"). While it may be the case that international courts and diplomatic organizations have good reasons to maintain specific and narrow definitions of what constitute wars, there are also good reasons to broaden the definition of "war," particularly where it can be shown that a war has a rate of casualties as large as the war on women, when the war is as global as the war on women, and where the state of war has continued for as long as humans have written records. Dierdre McPhillips recently offered an essay called "the war on women in five charts" that provides more statistical evidence (McPhillips, "War on Women").

There are no good grounds to rule out calling the systematic, millennia-old slaughter of women a war. It is an organized war grounded in powerful and ancient social systems for valuing persons, managing dowries and inheritances, and controlling family reproduction and lineages. It is a war encouraged by messages that objectify and dehumanize women. It is a war fostered by inducements to sexual predation, including pornography.

Lest anyone argue that the situation of women has improved, as this is being written on September 11, 2017, sixteen years after the attack on the World Trade Center in New York City, a CNN article featured a Namilia fashion show in New York in which all the dresses were covered in fabric reproductions of women's vulva (Feldma, "Lot of Vulvas Showing"). If the objectification and dehumanization of women is not already obvious enough, these clothes are designed to reinforce this message: "Look at me. You can reduce me to nothing but a vagina for your use." The questions to be addressed later are as follows: Is this a sign of progress, a breaking of a badly conceived "Victorian" social barrier? Or does this kind of pornography constitute an act of war? Is the suggestion that pornography could be an act of war puritanical or prudish? Is that truly an outrageous suggestion in the face of 330 million dead women compared to 250 million killed in all the wars, mass starvations, and civil wars of the twentieth century? Suppose the Nazis had run a fashion show of Jewish women wearing dresses covered in yellow stars of David? Would that not be viewed as a kind of war crime or at least an inducement to violence? However, is Namilia's fashion show just a playful ploy for attention? What kind of mental gymnastics are involved in choosing to view public pornography as a normal and healthy freedom of expression rather than as a prompt to objectify and dehumanize women on the street, in the workplace, and wherever else women may be met?

If one grants, however, that there is indeed a war against women, does it follow that the casualties of that war are victims of genocide?

Does the War Against Women Constitute Genocide?

Early in this project, Catharine MacKinnon cautioned me to be careful with formal definitions, because while everyone has a right to her or his own language, there are accepted international definitions of terms such as genocide. The focus of this section is the official United Nations definition of genocide, as published by the Office of the UN Special Adviser on the Prevention of Genocide, though the Rome Statute of the International Criminal Court will be addressed at the end of the chapter. The United Nations definition was adopted in 1948, and it includes: "any of the following acts committed with intent to destroy, in whole or in part, a national, ethnical, racial or religious group, as such: killing members of the group; causing serious bodily or mental harm to members of the group; deliberately inflicting on the group conditions of life calculated to bring about its physical destruction in whole or in part; imposing measures intended to prevent births within the group; forcibly transferring children of the group to another group" ("United Nations Office on Genocide Prevention"). This definition does not include gender as a defining characteristic of a protected group. To repeat, women are not a group according to the accepted definition of genocide. At issue here is whether this definition should be changed, as well as whether the definition and its longer framework are fatally flawed by simultaneously excluding women as a group while including a myriad of explanations and criteria that explicitly apply and refer to women as a group. The UN definition is radically inconsistent and self-contradictory as it stands.

Consider first how women fit into the basic definition. Three hundred thirty million members of this group were killed in the twentieth century. "Serious bodily and mental harm" was inflicted on members of this group by rape, fear of rape and sexual assault, genital mutilation, and other means. Conditions of life were deliberately—with planning and forethought—inflicted on members of this group "to bring about its physical destruction in part." Gynecide does not attempt to kill all women; that would be self-defeating. It does aim in many cultures to reduce the number of female children and to manage an economic problem posed by unwanted brides whose dowries would otherwise need to be repaid. Systematic rape by members of armies and other ethnic groups are "intended to prevent births" within the group. The language of this criterion, of course, is meant to apply to women as members of an ethnic or national group, not to women as women. Is it too much of a stretch to say that when rape (including rape by bayonets and other weapons) is directed against large numbers of women, the crime is directed not merely at women as members of a specific ethnic or national group (Congolese, Rwandans, Hutus, or Tutsis, for example), but that the violence is also and perhaps sometimes primarily directed at women because they are women?

The UN document expands these criteria in eight sections of commentary. In terms of factors that are relevant to genocide, it cites "tensions" with regard to "power and economic relations." Consider only the current situation in the United States of America: the differential between male and female pay, the absence of women in positions of leadership in corporations, the small numbers of women in elected positions, and the failure of the country to ratify an Equal Rights Amendment certainly are evidence of tension over power and economic relations. The reader may think that this merely states the obvious, that the obvious is something that is not important, or that the obvious is something beyond remedy.

Throughout this book, the point is to state many facts that are obvious in order to name the elephant in the room, the crime that is hiding in plain sight. It may also be reasonably objected from time to time that women themselves choose certain roles, that they choose careers that pay less, that they accept particular definitions of motherhood and family support that remove them from other economic activities. This author completed a study of women's careers at his own university (Sequeira et al., "Kingdom Has Not Yet Come"). While the status of female professors was not as dire as might have been expected, when women were asked about the long delays in their rise to full professor, or their relatively lower pay, they tended to produce the familiar rationalizations. They had chosen to delay because of responsibilities to their homes and families. While their answers were probably true, they stopped short of examining what forces within their families made those choices imperative or what the university could have done to assist women to prosper and to rise to more positions of leadership.

Besides, to these reasonable objections, the reply here and later will be that the best possible systems of discrimination operate by enlisting the cooperation of those who are victimized by discrimination, by persuading them that it is safer to go along with the way things are, and to persuade them as well to teach their children to obey the rules. Any study of prejudice and discrimination will find how powerfully and insidiously these forces operate to maintain unjust systems.

The UN document states that discrimination includes "compulsory identification of members of a particular group." This and other details will be explored in more detail during the review of Gregory Stanton's eight stages of genocide. Here it should be sufficient to point out that there are still laws in many countries that prescribe codes of dress to women. Recently in the US Congress there was a dispute over a rule that women working in or for the US Congress should not wear clothes that left their arms bare (Zengerle, "Right to Bare Arms"). Some Arab nations require women to cover their bodies and faces. Stop and consider the last sentences. In both the United States Congress and in Saudi Arabia, it was forbidden for women to have bare arms. There is a lively dialogue among conservative Christian groups on the Internet concerning whether the Bible bans women from wearing pants. Other nations fine women for wearing slacks, as in a 2009 case in Sudan, where a woman was fined two hundred dollars for wearing pants, but spared a public whipping (Gettleman, "Sudan Court Fines Woman"). A fine of two hundred dollars is a serious matter in a nation where the per capita GDP is less than $4,500 ("CIA Factbook—Sudan").

The UN document notes "imposition of taxes/fines" as one criterion for genocide. Globally, women are subject to various controls on marriage and birth control, and it is common in some countries for women to be killed if they break these rules. The International Honour Based Violence network estimates that there are five thousand honor killings each year. "Systematic exclusion of groups from positions of power" is another criterion. American women gained the franchise in 1920, as did British women. French women could not vote until 1945; Swiss women until the 1970s; Omani women until 2003 ("Timeline of Women's Suffrage"). Systematic exclusion from professions is another criterion. Consider when women were allowed to obtain college educations, to enroll in medical schools, and to enter other male preserves. As for fines, there is an ongoing debate in the United States as to whether any federal money should be provided for abortions, and a similar debate as to whether employers should be required to provide families with birth control as part of medical insurance. Conservatives have argued that it is important to respect the religious convictions of employers that do not approve of birth control. When families (when women) are forced to pay for birth control that is routinely provided by most employers, it is at least conceivable to consider the imposition of an extra expense on those women a "fine" for holding to a view of sexuality that differs from the convictions of their employers.

The UN states that there should be "overt justification for such discriminatory practices." Many churches in the United States and elsewhere continue to use passages from the Bible to deny women leadership roles in churches, to insist that they are wards of their husbands, and to enforce other limitations on women's participation in society. One would not need to look deep into history to find the arguments presented against women obtaining the right to vote. Again, Mr. Roy Moore, 2017 Alabaman candidate for the US Senate, has stated that the country would be better off without most of the amendments to the US Constitution, including the one that granted the vote to women (Peoples and Chandler, "Moore Denies Sexual Misconduct"; Moran, "Bill Maher"). One could dismiss this remark as an aberration. However, the lack of outcry within much of his state suggests that there must still be a deep willingness to return to some old and traditional society in which women have no rights and perhaps some people are returned to slavery.

The texts of other major religions are used in the same way to limit women's freedoms. In other words, there are and have been many "overt" and published justifications for discriminating against women. "Significant disparities in socioeconomic indicators" certainly include the abundant evidence for the glass ceiling and for women's lower pay. A "history of genocide or related serious and massive human rights violations" is a criterion, though a circular one because it defines genocide by asking for evidence of genocide. Since the point of this review is to show that women should be a group for the purposes of this definition, it should be relevant that there are "related serious and massive human rights violations" that have extended for at least four thousand years in the form of systematic killing of women for various cultural reasons. The United Nations criteria also call for evidence of denial. So far, the authorities that adopt definitions of genocide have not seen fit to include women among the targeted. What could be a greater denial than to leave women as a group out of the definition of groups that are subject to genocide?

Do women have "genuine access to the protection afforded by the [political and legal] structures?" Do women have a history of being believed when they claim they have been raped? Hardly. Is there evidence of "patterns of impunity and lack of accountability?" In 2016, a Stanford student was sentenced to six months for raping a member of the Stanford swimming team who was unconscious at the time (Stack, "Light Sentence"). The young man's father made remarks to the effect that his son had only inconvenienced the woman for about fifteen minutes. The sentence was below that typically given for rape. Many challenged the judge's sentence and pointed out that this was a clear case of impunity and lack of accountability for a serious crime committed against a woman.

The United Nations considers evidence of genocide to include "depiction of a targeted group as dangerous." One of the obstacles to electing a female president in the United States has been explicit (or more recently implicit) statements that women have times of the month when their temperaments cannot be trusted, and therefore they are unfit to serve because they might make dangerous errors of judgment. During President Trump's campaign, he made comments about how disgusting it was that women bled from everywhere. A "sudden increase in inflammatory rhetoric or hate propaganda" is another sign of genocide. Trump's election has been followed by an increase in many kinds of inflammatory rhetoric and hate propaganda, as well as by the pink pussy hat marches to protest his leadership. The president issued many "statements amounting to hate speech" with respect to women, as well as with respect to other groups such as Hispanics, Mexicans, and Muslims (Kertscher, "Allegations about Donald Trump").

The UN criteria list among "obvious" signs of "the crime of genocide" such factors as "killings, abduction and disappearances, torture, rape and sexual violence." Catharine MacKinnon's work on the gynecide in Serbia and Bosnia meets all of these standards. So do the abduction of girls by Boko Haram in Nigeria and by the Lord's Army in Uganda and the Congo (Bouchaud, "Congo accuses Rwandan Army"; "DR Congo: Mass Rape in Goma Prison"; Mudiaki, "Goma, la trista capitale"; Kimani, "Les femmes du Congo"; Monanga, "Génocide en RDC"; Malagardis, "L'Afrique du sud malade"; Searcey, "They Fled Boko Haram"). In Serbia and Bosnia, to use the language of the United Nations criteria, there was "systematic rape of women . . . intended to transmit a new ethnic identity to the child or to cause humiliation and terror in order to fragment the group." Yazidi women kidnapped by ISIS troops came home with babies they did not want, feeling humiliated, and suffering from PTSD to the point of being in nearly catatonic states. They were victims of what the Swedes call "resignation syndrome," a condition diagnosed in many of the refugees who have come to that nation, including Yazidi refugees (Pressly, "Resignation Syndrome"). The condition has also been diagnosed among Holocaust survivors, including the Romany people. More recently, there is evidence that Libyan male victims of repeated sodomy are suffering from the same condition: reduced to lying in bed with no motivation to do anything after they have been released from prisons where they were sodomized on a daily basis with broomsticks and other instruments, sometimes being filmed (Allegra, "Subjugate Men"). In view of the global treatment of women, it is fair to ask whether this story of the torture of men received two-page spreads in both British and French papers because the focus of the torture is men.

Finally, the United Nations notes that the forces that trigger genocide can include "upcoming elections." It is still routine in many nations, including the United States, of course, to have public dialogues about the fitness of women for office or to note how special or unusual it is for a woman to rise to a particular role. Obviously, this was an issue in the 2016 US presidential elections, where Democratic vice-presidential candidate Senator Kaine remarked afterwards that it was uniquely difficult for a woman to run for president (Darby, "Tim Kaine's Response").

What is most remarkable about the United Nations criteria for genocide is a logical problem at their core. Women *as a group* are used to define genocide over and over again, and yet women *as a group* are not included in the official list of groups to whom genocide may occur. Gender is not, according to the United Nations, a defining characteristic for genocide, except that in the case of women, it is in fact a defining characteristic of genocide. If one wanted to play with Bertrand Russell's famous paradox in set theory, one might say that in this case there is a set (female identity) that is used to define all other sets (elements of genocide and groups targeted by genocide), and yet that set (female identity) is not a set in itself. This is not logical. It is self-contradictory. It follows that the definitions of genocide offered by the United Nations are self-contradictory.

Should further evidence of the confusion in the UN definition be necessary, the United Nations itself publishes reports on the status of women in the world, such as the 2015 UN Report on Women, that devote entire chapters to violence against women, and the healthcare chapter emphasizes the problem that women in many nations do not receive adequate prenatal care, which of course puts them and their children at great risk (United Nations Statistic Division, "World's Women 2015"). UNICEF publishes its own annual report on women's health, which indicated in 2015 that maternal mortality had dropped by 50 percent since 1990, a staggering and wonderful decrease. Nevertheless, as of 2015, the nation with the highest maternal mortality rate, Sierra Leone, had a rate of 1,360 deaths per 100,000 live births, which was also calculated as a lifetime risk of about 6 percent that a mother would die in birth. Greece and Iceland reported the lowest rates, both 4 per 100,000 live births. For the United States, with a maternal mortality rate of 14 per 100,000 live births, this meant about a 0.01 percent chance of death per birth, or around 560 women dying in childbirth per year. Obviously not all maternal mortality is due to poor medical care, or national and local priorities that do not emphasize the health of pregnant women. To what extent in each nation is maternal mortality a function of a lower priority on women's health?

This ongoing genocide against women could be considered problematic, in the sense of not fitting definitions well, because it is not discrete in time and place, like the Hutu and Tutsi genocides of Rwanda or the genocide in the Congo that has lasted for over fifty years. It is not discrete, like the genocide in Bosnia and Serbia that is temporarily halted, though the nations in that region maintain many closed borders and it may be that the trafficking in women's bodies and even in human organs (largely begun during the war) is continuing. The genocide against women is not discrete like the Holocaust, though anti-Semitism and killings of Jews continue routinely. It is not discrete like the conflict between Black Africans and Berbers in Mauritania that has lasted for centuries, or the conflict between Arabs and Black Africans in the Sahel, in Darfur, and in the surrounding regions.

These examples are used to make a fundamental point: genocide is probably not discrete. Genocide is an expression of hatreds and conflicts that have lasted for generations, if not centuries or millennia. It is not geographically isolated, either, though there may be outbreaks in geographically limited areas. Of course, neither are genocide or discrimination against people because of their religion or race geographically limited. Racism and anti-Semitism are not geographically or temporally limited. Moreover, the genocide against women does not necessarily involve large masses of men breaking out of neighborhoods to kill every woman they find, in the way that some national and community genocides involve outbursts of mass killing. Instead, the genocide against women achieves its extraordinary

totals of deaths by means of daily, routine killings of infants, brides, prostitutes, battered women, raped women, victims of serial killers, victims
of substandard medical care, and other causes. On the other hand, there
are indeed many recent instances in which gangs of men have singled out
women of various ethnic and religious groups for gang rape and murder.
The situation calls for a change in the definitions or in the assumptions we
make about how genocide happens and how it is carried out (United Nations, "Annual Review 2003"; "Annual Review 2016").

Finally, one might reasonably object that what has been presented
here is a case that there is an ongoing "crime against humanity" that targets
women rather than "genocide." The technical difference is evidence of "intent" to destroy a group. There is no evidence that anyone wants to destroy
all women, because then there would no longer be reproduction. On the
other hand, there is clear evidence of intent to kill millions of women in
those nations that engage in female infanticide. What about the killing of
women in those cultures where there is not such a long history of infanticide or bride murder? What about the women who die in childbirth? If a
country decides not to provide adequate medical care to pregnant women
in the face of other priorities, is there any intent to discard a certain number
of women who will die giving birth? Can one make a case that there is adequate evidence of "intent" to target women? What is proposed here is the
following criterion: if the global treatment of women shows that women are
systematically and permanently subjected to most or all of Gregory Stanton's eight stages of genocide, then that constitutes sufficient evidence that
the intent is genocidal. Moreover, the distinction between crimes against
humanity and genocide feels somewhat artificial, as if the intent of those
who make such distinctions is to define genocide as the highest level of
crime and then find a way to define most of the mass killing as something
less than real genocide because the killers have not expressed intent in
the right way. To repeat a point made earlier, this is like American courts
maintaining that the national system of justice is not racist, in spite of vast
statistical evidence, because one cannot find written documents, or audio-
or videotapes of judges and jury members explicitly stating that they intend
to treat people of some racial backgrounds more harshly.

Nevertheless, using the definitions provided by the United Nations
itself, it is clear that women as a group are the targets of ongoing genocide.
The point of the sections that follow is to underline how well the situation of women in the world fits one well-accepted set of definitions of how

genocide takes places in stages, the stages articulated by Gregory Stanton's Genocide Watch. These eight stages constitute a rational taxonomy of what takes place as groups of people are targeted. While other lists of stages are possible, it would be difficult to contest the accuracy of Stanton's observations.

chapter two

THE STAGES OF GENOCIDE

The Eight Stages of Genocide

THE POINT OF THIS book is to look at what we already know, but to do so from a particular perspective so that the weight of the knowledge becomes apparent and perhaps will be sufficient to motivate change. Throughout, the examples for genocidal activities will be drawn as much as possible from current trends and traditions. It is obvious enough that in the past women were the property of their husbands, could not work, could not attend colleges, could not serve in professions, could not vote, had limited control over their assets, and were limited in a myriad of other ways. The question now is how much of this apparatus of discrimination still operates, even in the most "advanced" societies.

Gregory Stanton's Genocide Watch lists eight stages of genocide (Stanton, "8 Stages of Genocide"). After reviewing them briefly here, each will be explored in somewhat more detail to emphasize the power of the forces at work. First people are classified. This is normal. It is impossible to walk the streets of any city without noticing that there are men and women, that some people have lighter skins, that some people wear clothing that suggests citizenship of particular nations or their relative wealth. Some people, after the election of Barack Obama, dreamed that the United States was entering a post-racial period. It is not likely that there will ever be a time when people simply don't notice at all that there are differences of that social construction called race. One meets people from time to time who are convinced that, after living in Asia or Africa, they mean what they say when they assert that they no longer noticed people's racial identities. What we know about that knapsack of racial privilege suggests that if those observers had been stripped of all their privileges as people from a dominant economic culture, they would readily have begun to notice racial, political, social, and economic distinctions as a matter of basic survival and of negotiating the transactions of daily life (National SEED Project, "White Privilege").

According to Stanton, people are next associated with specific symbols, such as dress or cultural attributes, or the long noses that are supposed to distinguish Semitic peoples, whether Arab or Jew. A brief tour of racist websites will re-introduce anyone to all of the typical symbols. One of my neighbors in the fully white Southern California suburb where I grew up later became an American ex-patriot and a stateless person who has been convicted by a German court of Holocaust denial and who maintains a racist website that advocates killing refugees that attempt to enter Europe. His site is a compendium of the kinds of images and stereotypes one might find promulgated by any hate group. I will not give his name or his website; that kind of material is widely available. I mention his case because any one of us can be surprised to find such attitudes arising in unexpected places. In the case of women, anyone driving down the road will see pickups that have mud guards that feature, in bright chrome, silhouettes of women with enormous breasts, lush and abundant hair, tiny waistlines, and carefully modeled legs. For example, in 2017, the BBC reported that a restaurant in China posted a sign offering discounts to women based on the size of their bras, with specific correlations between cup size and percentages off their meals ("Chinese Restaurants").

Third, groups of people are dehumanized by objectification. One is taught by campaigns of dehumanization to see members of a group as mere objects that must be eliminated, cleared away, washed away, and/or expunged. This stage of genocide presents challenges, in the sense that it may not be easy to find images of girl babies or unwanted brides who have been objectified symbolically. Are there images in China that reinforce the importance of killing unwanted female babies? In my own experience, I recall a Chinese neighbor in the United States whose Chinese parents in Hong Kong responded with an interesting symbol to the news that my neighbor had given birth to a second girl. The grandparents sent a pair of brown boys' pants as a baby gift. The objectification was complex in this way: the symbol indicated that the proper kind of news was the birth of a boy, and that was the only news that would be accepted. The news of a girl's birth was not noticed at all; the girl baby was symbolically expunged. This was a case not of objectification, but rather of refusal to recognize that there was an "object," that is to say, a baby girl, at all. That baby girl, I am proud to say, is now an attorney working for an international advocacy agency in the District of Columbia. Andrea Dworkin and others have articulated masterfully how women are often reduced to nothing but vaginas (e.g., Dworkin, *Life and Death*).

From a philosophical perspective, objectification means, in Martin Buber's terms, viewing a person as an It rather than a Thou, so that the relationship to that person becomes an I-It relationship rather than an I-Thou relationship (Buber, *I and Thou*). Or, in terms of Immanuel Kant's view of ethics, to objectify a person means to view a person as merely a means to an end, as something expendable, as, for example, a means to achieve a sexual release. The alternative is to see the other as an end in herself, as a full person whose own objectives, desires, and meaning are to be honored and cultivated (Kant, *Perpetual Peace*). A very simple test of the ethical emptiness of pornography is to ask the question of whether this image or description invites the viewer to experience this woman as a means to an end or as an end in herself; does this image or description invite the viewer to enter into an I-Thou relationship or into an I-It relationship?

Precisely how did customs such as dowry and bride price arise? Is a woman without value, so that when one gets rid of her, there must be a payment to the family that receives her? Or is a woman an item of value that must be purchased by a husband? Either way, and whatever the origins of these traditions, women are reduced to commodities.

Fourth, there are organized efforts to limit the lives of those in targeted groups. I think of when my wife was told by a Berkeley history professor that the department did not think much of admitting women to doctoral study, because women just had babies and dropped out. This was in 1968, a year when one expected something different from faculty at an institution renowned for its liberalism and progressiveness. I think as well of a friend who was the first woman admitted to the association of Freudian psychologists in Seattle, after a mighty effort to challenge the sexism of the group. More contemporary examples will be offered later. Leaving anecdotes aside, while organized efforts to prepare for genocide typically involve such steps as the development of political parties and ethnic organizations to enforce discrimination and later mass killing, the community organizing against women is found in such common measures as denying women the right to vote; to wear certain clothing; to enter schools or work in specific professions; to drive cars (a rule just recently changed in Saudi Arabia); to hold jobs at all, as in Saudi Arabia; or to serve in leadership positions (either business-related or religious). The glass ceiling is a result of deliberate organization deeply embedded in social learning. As for organizations designed to exclude and to diminish women, it would be easy to list a legion of men's clubs, sports associations, religious fraternities, and other associations whose exclusivity with respect to gender includes either an implicit or explicit message of prejudging and diminishing female humans.

Fifth, there is systematic polarization, in the form of public events and publicity to emphasize the difference between the targeted group and the ruling group. In the case of women, however, there is a degree of gender polarization so extreme that one hardly notices it. The late Sandra Bern wrote extensively about the sociology of gender polarization, which can be seen everywhere in the differences between male and female clothing, jewelry, shoes, hair styles and length, social standards for excellence and body shape, muscle development, career possibilities, and of course the long history of ways in which women have been excluded from careers and participation in public life. It is hard to think of a culture in which this polarization is not both evident and extreme. Perhaps the people described in Fyodor Gladkov's Soviet Realist novel *Cement* overcame some gender polarization, wearing the same drab workers' clothes, living in group housing, sending their children off to be raised by the state. In that book, every citizen is so dedicated to building a cement factory for the Soviet State that nothing else is important. Catharine MacKinnon's analysis of the conflicts between Marxism and feminism, however, may expose the lie in this idealistic reading of Gladkov (MacKinnon, *Toward a Feminist Theory*). In the United States during World War II, Rosie the Riveter broke the mold for symbolizing women, not only because she was a woman working in industry during World War II, but also because she is shown in the famous poster flexing her biceps while wearing loose fitting work clothes without any adornment and a head scarf that obliterates (or does it enhance?) any art in the way she wears her hair. More will be said of this later. Here it is worth thinking merely about women's shoes and their common lack of utility and practicality: they are designed to make it hard to walk, hard to defend oneself, hard to flee. Many women's shoes are the technological equivalent of Chinese foot binding.

To be fair to men, societies are organized to separate and polarize men, too. Much of the genocide related to pornography takes place in wars and civil wars, and the warriors are mostly men who have been taken from their normal surroundings, trained to some degree, and then forced to participate in violent activities that they may not have chosen and that leaves many of them profoundly damaged. Armies are polarized because they include few women. About 15 percent of the American military is female ("Women in the United States Army"). The French military is 15.5 percent female (Ministère des Armées, "Femmes dans l'armée français"). Data on other nations indicate an increasing number of women in the military and more nations willing to place women in combat. Still, military forces are to a large degree segregated and polarized by gender ("Women in the Military by Country"; "Women in the United States Army"). Of course, this segregation is also accompanied by sexual harassment and assaults within military services.

Sixth, there is preparation for genocide. In the case of current infanticide in China, there is controversy about what is currently taking place. The United Nations' estimates for future missing women indicate an expectation that infanticide will continue at present rates. Others have argued that China's one-child policy aggravated the problem and that a change in that policy will make a difference. However, the practice of infanticide is very ancient, as histories show (Mungello, *Drowning Girls in China*). It was common to keep a box of ashes under the birthing bed for suffocating infants; drowning in a bucket of water was another method. Preparing these devices and methods was preparation for genocide. In the anglophone world, there are many bodies of evidence for various forms of infanticide. Gilbert and Sullivan's operetta *H.M.S. Pinafore* features Buttercup, the woman who switched two infants. She confesses to having been a "baby farmer," a role that generally meant a woman who was hired to dispose of unwanted infants. Daniel Defoe's title character Roxana carries on at length about how good she felt that the baby farmers she hired for her unwanted children actually raised them, when she certainly knew that the whole point of the tradition was to pay a small sum of money to a stranger with the spoken agreement that the child would be raised to adulthood, while the unspoken understanding was that the stranger would kill the child immediately in exchange for the payment (Defoe, *Roxana*). Laws were passed in the American colonies to keep parents from sleeping with newborns, because it was understood that parents could "accidentally on purpose" roll over on an unwanted baby and suffocate it during the night. There are, in addition, many examples of group activities that have the function of preparing men to mistreat women. Several will be discussed later.

Seventh, there is the genocidal activity itself. While soldiers in Bosnia and Serbia carried out systematic rape and murder of women, arriving in tanks covered with pornographic pictures, the situation is no less terrible in places like the Congo, where rebel groups arrive in towns and requisition the girls for use as sex objects and as laborers ("Epidemie du viols"; Jones, "Congo"; Kakutani, "King Leopold's Ghost"; Batha, "Ravaged by Ebola"). As will be seen later, while boys who are kidnapped and forced to fight are sometimes rescued, only a tiny percentage of dragooned girls is ever recovered because they tend to be hidden deep in the bush rather than found after battles in the open. Eighth is denial, such as the UN denial that women constitute a group subject to genocide; or, perversely, the news reports at the time of Hugh Hefner's death repeating that he did not think of *Playboy* as a sex magazine. So many people, of course, explained that they subscribed solely because of the quality of the journalism.

One need not reflect long to realize that six or more of these stages are constantly taking place with respect to the lives of women in developed nations, as well as in underdeveloped nations. The first two stages are, in a sense, natural. It is not possible to be color-blind with respect to "racial" difference, for example, though race itself is a cultural construct. Everyone takes into consideration the visual cues that convey information about gender, race, and socio-economic status. Harvard Implicit Prejudice tests assume that of course everyone will be able to see the difference between a black face and a white face; what the test looks for is the way that subjects control any tendencies to associate racial identity with pre-judgments about goodness and badness ("Take a Test—Project Implicit"). While I have not studied the underlying assumptions of the tests, my judgment from taking them is that the test-builders must also have assumed that all of us bear some form of prejudice, that whites have for the most part picked up some tendencies to feel prejudice against non-whites, and that non-whites have also learned to be suspicious or prejudiced against whites. The test therefore looks for our ability to manage our complex and pervasive social programming by avoiding snap judgments based on our perceptions of racial differences.

We also choose symbols that represent us, and fashion magazines and advertisements encourage both men and women to choose clothing and accessories that emphasize masculinity, femininity, and sexuality. Objectification and dehumanization naturally follow. At issue here is the extent to which the objectification of women is an industrial product, a system of images and expectations and permissions to abuse delivered on an industrial scale. Of course, this has gone on for millennia. The point is to ask whether, in face of those 330 million dead and counting, one might imagine a world in which the relations between the genders were significantly less dangerous. Women are also the target of constant preparation for genocide. Polarization of the genders is constant. Rituals of preparation for genocide, especially rituals of preparation for rape, are very common throughout the world. The last stages of genocide are the killing (or the other actions) that are the equivalent of killing a community, followed by denial that anything happened at all. While some of these stages are so obvious as to require little comment, an examination of how they are discussed in the world turns out to reveal unexpected similarities among common community rituals and highly dangerous deliberate preparations for assault. In fact, many cultures appear to accept an extraordinary level of preparation and assault without much comment. The next sections dig into the eight stages in somewhat more detail.

Classification

The act of classifying often entails attaching a value judgment. The words "womanish" and "effeminate" do not merely indicate the female gender of *homo sapiens*. Those words also mean that the persons who have those characteristics are also weak or lacking in some way. A manly man is a good man; a womanish man is weak. An effeminate woman, even, means an excessive degree of feminine attributes.

While one could examine many ways in which the genders are classified in current human cultures, to cut to the chase, women are classified as victims. The first page of the *Seattle Times* on November 13, 2017, led off with an article by Sara Jean Green titled "Strangulation is a Powerful Tool of Violence That Often Leaves No Physical Mark: Officials in King Count Want It Noticed, Prosecuted." The article explained that in the spectrum of domestic violence, strangulation tended to be the last step before murder, and that the county medical examiner and other authorities were determined to carry out a campaign of education and activism to address widespread cases of strangulation. The article stated that "second degree assault by strangulation is the most frequently filed domestic violence charge in King County Superior Court." King County is home to the city of Seattle and to many leading technology firms; it is a sophisticated and generally progressive place. To make its point literally graphic, the article continued with a full-page spread of a woman's head, identifying relevant sections of the brain, the trachea, the hyoid bone, the jugular vein and carotid artery, and other anatomical structures damaged during strangulation. A cynic might call the article a guide to how to strangle. On reflection, it is extraordinary that a major American urban newspaper would need to publish a general warning against the dangers of strangling a woman during a domestic dispute. On further reflection, the article is a statement that women are likely victims: that is their identity, their classification. To state the relatively obvious, on the following day, *Le Monde* featured an essay by Deborah Epstein, a professor of law at Georgetown University, explaining that "the majority of mass murders are made by men who have committed domestic violence" (my translation). There is a link between the classification of women as victims and the commission of mass violence against women as a group.

Symbolization

"I moved on her like a bitch," said the soon-to-be-president of the United States in a notorious recording released a month before the election ("Transcript: Donald Trump's Taped Comments"). A webpage called "Female of the Species" lists a number of animal names to call women (though it leaves out fox). Those included are bat, bird, bitch, bunny, cat, chick, cow, crow, dog, filly, fishwife, harridan, hen, mare, shrew, and vixen. No doubt a study of languages other than English would provide many more.

Definitions of the words "metonymy" and "synecdoche" differ slightly. These two figures of speech define many of the ways that women are symbolized, classified, and dehumanized. A synecdoche is a figure of speech in which a part indicates the whole, or the whole indicates the part, as when one uses the term for genitalia to indicate the whole person or vice versa. A metonym, however, uses the name of something related to indicate an object. Animal names for women are perhaps metonyms, because they are meant to indicate aspects of femininity by comparing those attributes to those of animals. A frisky filly, for example, or a wildly reproductive rabbit. Symbolization reduces something to an object by which it can be referenced with ease. Like dehumanization, it is objectification, though symbols can of course be honorific rather than demeaning.

Dehumanization

"It's so fundamental to the female experience to be mistreated and feel ashamed of it." So said actress Jennifer Lawrence in the days following the decision of the film academy to expel Harvey Weinstein from its membership because of the increasing evidence of his sexual predation (Delbyck, "Jennifer Lawrence Recalls"). Gretchen Carlson, who filed a suit against Fox News CEO Roger Ailes before he was forced to leave his post, added that the Weinstein case was a "tipping point," as reported by the *Huffington Post* (Vagianos, "Gretchen Carlson on Harvey Weinstein"). Sexual harassment in the film or any other industry is hardly surprising, though the willingness to make that harassment a public issue is promising, if it leads to change. Parsing Ms. Lawrence's comment, she is saying that it is fundamental to being a woman to be mistreated, which is dehumanizing in itself. Then she adds, importantly, that it is fundamental as well to experience shame because one has been mistreated. Shame, not anger. Which means that the burden is placed upon the victim of the abuse. That this is a common reaction by those who are abused does not reduce the importance of the observation. Actress Reese Witherspoon echoed Ms. Lawrence's view: that it is fundamental to female humanity to be ashamed of what one is (France, "Reese Witherspoon"). She explained, further, that part of her shame came from being forced to line up naked with other aspiring actresses and to be filmed, apparently for evaluation. This is similar to the stories of Mr. Trump visiting the dressing rooms at his Miss Universe contest, because he was in charge, and viewing many naked contestants as they changed their clothes for parts of the competition (Covert, "Trump Bragged"). Identical allegations were made with respect to his intrusiveness at the Miss Teen USA contest, where the women were ages fifteen and sixteen, according to Tom Kertscher's report in *Politifact* (Kertscher, "Allegations about Donald Trump"). The idea of inspecting naked women is similar to images of naked Jews awaiting their "showers" at Nazi death camps. First you are stripped and examined, and then you are abused or killed. You are reduced to so much flesh, like cattle in a pen before they are herded into the killing chute.

The primary means of dehumanizing women are objectifying them by reducing them to some fraction of themselves. That part may be to serve as nothing but a means of reproduction and family service, a sex object, genitalia or some other anatomical feature, or a sales target. Many sites, such as The Gender Ads Project, provide ample evidence of the ways that women are dehumanized by advertising of all kinds that reduces them to sexual objects. William Brennan's essay on the semantics of dehumanizing women fills out the picture, to cite just one analysis (Brennan, "Female Objects").

To put the issue in Kant's terms, dehumanization is treating a human female as a means to an end rather than as an end in herself. To think of a woman as just a womb, or a vagina, or a house servant, or an object that can fulfill a purpose for someone else, is to dehumanize her. The late Andrea Dworkin wrote often of her terrible violation in a New York jail by a pair of prison doctors (Dworkin, *Life and Death*). The following story of a friend serves a similar purpose, which is to detail the complexity and the multiple assaults involved in dehumanizing a woman. In the early seventies, when I worked in an Oakland hospital, one of my close friends was a young woman who worked as a receptionist in the same department. She was African American, married, the mother of two young boys, and a high school graduate. She was also bright, lively, and deeply intelligent. She read Sylvia Plath's *The Bell Jar* when it came out and reflected on her own life in the context of Plath's book. My friend spoke often about the ways in which she was humiliated. Not only was she black and female, but she had also been poor and on welfare when she gave birth to her two sons. Now she and her husband had dependable jobs, though they did not pay well, and they lived in a largely African American housing complex in Albany, up the bay from Oakland. One memory that haunted her that she needed to talk about frequently, as difficult as that was, concerned how she had been required, as a condition of receiving obstetric care from the state, to be a subject for gynecological examinations by medical students. This may not be a current practice. Physicians I have consulted, who were trained at about the same time, one of them in the Bay Area, were surprised and even shocked by her story. My friend had traumatic memories of being reduced to an object in multiple ways. There was her race, her gender, her poverty that labeled her as a failure, her youth, her pregnant state, and the way she was put on display, literally splayed out to be viewed and probed by groups of strangers learning details of the female anatomy, of pregnancy, and of the birthing process. Any one of the labels attached to her served to take away some of her humanity; she had experienced a cascade of labels and experiences that reduced her to a sexual object.

In the weeks before I left this job to travel and to pursue graduate studies, my friend became cold and distant. I asked her what had changed, and she said, frankly and helpfully, that I was going on to travel the world, get a PhD, become a professor, and so much else, while her life was going to be just what it was then, sitting behind a window working as a receptionist. She had the potential to do so much more, and to a degree that cannot be calculated, she was choosing to hold herself back, though what I am still not capable of understanding fully is the extent to which all of those labels put on her, her blackness, her femininity, her impoverished upbringing, her motherhood and responsibilities, and the trauma of her experiences would hold her back from any bold move to free herself from what she considered her fate. So far as I know, she was right. I have not contacted her directly. However, the intrusive Internet allows us all now to collect so much information, from which I have gleaned that she returned to the city where she was born, continued to work in hospitals, and is surrounded by a large and (I hope) supportive family. As she predicted, I became a professor, traveled, taught, wrote, and all the rest, much of that due to the fact that I am male and white. The point of her story is that dehumanization may take many forms, and that dehumanization can be the result of a multitude of assaults and labels, rather than a single cause. Such dehumanization becomes a huge leaden weight that can keep a woman from rising as far as her talent and intelligence would normally guarantee. I made a point of telling her story to many classes and of dedicating sections of my course on American ethnic literature to her and her wisdom.

Organization

A good example of organization leading to rape and genocide is the sometimes subtle, sometimes contradictory system of messages, community organizations, and political parties that are currently pursuing an agenda of making India a fully Hindu nation (Atal and Kosambi, *Violence Against Women*; Banerjee, *Make Me a Man*; Vahini, "Inside an Indian Camp"; Vishva Hindu Parishad, "Durga Vahini"; Singh, Kanishka; Venugopal, "What Does It Take"). The intent of this movement is to eliminate the presence of non-Hindu groups in India, particularly Christians and Muslims. The movement also aims to inculcate fundamentalist Hindu beliefs and a return to many traditional gender roles. The movement has enormous power because the present Prime Minister of India, Narendra Modi, is a member and now leader of the BJP party, and has been accused on several occasions, both as prime minister and in his previous political roles, of helping to organize pogroms against Muslims and other groups. He has been formally exonerated of those charges by Indian political panels, though the judgment of those panels has been challenged by other groups (Chaturvedi, "Modi Must End").

The Bharatiya Janata Party, or the BJP, is associated with two community movements. The Rashtrya Swayamsevak Sangh (RSS) trains young men in Hindu principles, martial arts skills, and a largely traditional view of the roles of women. In the training camps, the men dress in brown shirts and shorts, carry long sticks, and are both indoctrinated and prepared to fight (Venugopal, "What Does It Take"). Sikata Banerjee, in her 2005 study *Make Me a Man! Masculinity, Hinduism and Nationalism in India,* describes the way that the RSS creates a particular view of Hindu manliness, while at the same time promoting a view of a woman as a "heroic mother, chaste wife, and celibate, masculinized warrior." This view of women is a curious combination of a traditional wife who obeys her husband and a warrior prepared to attack non-Hindu groups ("रणरागिणी शाखेच्या"; Sanyai, "After UP's 'Anti-Romeo Squad'"). The women are organized and trained in their own camps into groups of Durga Vahini, or "Army of Durga," who operate as a "moral police" squad, according to an article by Smita Gupta (Gupta, "Durga Vahini"). Roving groups of Durga Vahini look for and capture men who are misbehaving in public, and then turn them in to the police for prosecution (Nashrullah, "Militant Hindu Camp"). The women are trained to fight obscenity and human trafficking. In a BBC report, an Army of Durga militant explained that the women "must be strong enough to break the bones of the enemy but docile enough to never question their husbands." The enemy, the article made clear, comprises Christians and Muslims, though it also includes Hindu men who disrespect women in public.

At the same time, male leaders of the BJP party have been known to make highly offensive remarks about women and rape. According to one article in *Indian Express*, during discussion of a bill against rape, a party leader said that boys must be able to "follow" girls, though it is not clear what "follow" meant or implied (Khan). Did it mean shadow, accost, even disrespect women in public, or rape those who were out alone at night? The same party leaders made many remarks about female candidates for office, calling those with lighter skins more attractive and naming unattractive female candidates. Another article about the same controversy, reported by the BBC, took a nuanced while offensive view of rape. On the one hand, the legislator was reported as saying that pornography was responsible for rape, which indicates some level of understanding of the dynamics of rape. On the other hand, the legislator said that "boys" should not be hanged for making a mistake, implying that rape was often just an error. Babulal Guar, Home Minister of Madhya Pradesh State, was quoted as saying that "rape is a social crime . . . It is sometimes right and sometimes wrong." The article did not clarify the circumstances under which he thought that rape would be morally right ("Indian Politicians' 'Unfortunate' Rape Remarks").

Modi's party has been accused of complicity with many bloggers or trolls who attack his critics, sometimes with extremely pornographic comments about sex, sex with their mothers, and female genitalia (Press Trust of India, "Intl Experts Spoil Modi's Party").

These organized groups or their proxies, sometimes dressed in saffron robes, have carried out raids against Christian and Muslim communities ("2002 Gujarat Riots"; India United Against Fascism, "India: The BJP"; "2008 Khandamal Nun Gang-Rape Case"; "'Kandhamal Tells the Whole Story"; Mehtal, "Riots in Surat"). The legal cases have continued for over a decade following some of the incidents, with conflicting testimonies about whether the riots were started by the Hindus or the "enemies," whether the enemies bombed a train, whether the enemies butchered a sacred cow or whether the saffron gangs found a dead cow and paraded it around towns to incite anti-Muslim rioting. Bal Thackeray, a Hindu leader, was quoted saying that "Muslims are a cancer to this country."

Notable among these riots are two groups of incidents that occurred in Gujarat and in Kandhamal in Orisha. A 2013 essay in Opendemocracy. net includes an accusation that during the riots in Surat, part of Gujarat, Hindu mobs gang-raped Muslim women, filming the assaults with bright lights at a time when power had been cut off to most of the Muslim neighborhoods. The availability of electric power to light the filming of rapes of course suggests planning, as does cutting off the power to the neighborhoods under attack ("India: The BJP"). During the 2002 Gujarat riots, fighting continued in the city for three days, followed by three months of conflict in Ahmenabad, and a full year of sporadic anti-Muslim riots. The attacks were precipitated by an assault on a train full of Hindu pilgrims, though some witnesses say that attack was faked by Hindu extremists. Officially, 1,044 people were killed, and 100,000 Muslim homes were destroyed. *Indian Express* reported that "international experts spoil[ed] Modi's party" when they said that the attacks in "Gujarat [were] worse than Bosnia." In both cases, the paper stated, "sexual violence was being used as a strategy for terrorizing women belonging to a minority community" (Press Trust of India, "Intl Experts Spoil Modi's Party").

The violence in Christian areas of Orisha was similar. Radical Hindus in saffron robes attacked Christians and attempted to force them to convert back to Hinduism. One hundred Christians were officially reported dead, six thousand homes were destroyed, and fifty thousand people were displaced. The rioting included multiple gang rapes. *Times of India* reported on the conclusion of the trial of nine people charged with raping a Catholic nun. Three were convicted and six acquitted ("Viol et meurtre d'une religieuse").

Another system of organized violence against women in India is the dedication of women to temples, which is discussed later. Here it will serve to point out that there are temples in several parts of India where young girls are dedicated to permanent temple service by their parents, though in some cases girls are trafficked from other parts of the nations for this work. According to some accounts, the girls may be "initiated" (that is, raped) while their parents are still present in another part of the temple and can hear their child's protests. The girls serve the "needs" of both temple priests and of higher caste members of the community who pay for sex. In this case, there is a permanently organized system of abuse with prominent permanent locations and highly respected and powerful custodians of the premises.

These cases reveal the way in which Stanton's stages of genocide fade into one another. The leading political party of India, which currently controls the government, is directly associated with organizations that provide paramilitary training to both men and women. The members of these organizations are also radicalized and taught to hate Muslims and Christians, while at the same time learning to fight against obscenity, male sexual predators, and human traffickers. Both men and women are taught gender identities that reinforce traditional views of women, with strict female obedience to husbands, although the women are also taught to be warriors for Hinduism. Members of these groups appear to have filmed and distributed their own pornography in the course of attacks on other religious groups. Altogether, this is a highly organized and powerful system.

Pakistan, according to the Wikipedia site dedicated to a discussion of women's issues in that nation, is "one of the most dangerous countries in the world for women" ("Pakistan Female Infanticide"). The article does not specify which nations are more dangerous, although a recent poll by the Thomas Reuters Foundation, drawing on over two hundred experts, judged that the most dangerous countries for women were, in rank order, Afghanistan, the Democratic Republic of the Congo, Pakistan, India, and Somalia (Goldsmith, "Factbox"). A brief scan of Pakistan's political history over the last fifty years shows that while there has been some progress toward more freedom for women, that progress has been halting, and to a large extent it depends on changes in the central government. At best, the situation appears to be one in which the current levels of progress are routinely imperiled. The institutional groundwork of the controls on women has consisted of two highly organized government structures. First, there is the existence of a dual judicial system, with a civil justice system and then a Federal Sharia Court that has the power to challenge legislation and that applies Islamic principles when making its decisions ("Federal Sharia Court Pakistan"). As in the case of the US Supreme Court, much depends on the philosophical and judicial leanings of those appointed to serve in this court, and while civil jurists have outnumbered religious representatives for some time, that weighting of the court is not guaranteed to continue. Recently this court has taken up a challenge to a law passed by the Parliament of Pakistani that would protect women in the Punjab against violence.

Second, there are the Hudood Ordinances, which placed many limitations on women, with the first laws introduced in 1977 and somewhat moderated in 1979 ("Hudood Ordinances"). While these have been gradually tempered by later administrations, many of the ordinances still stand. Under these ordinances, to cite one notorious example, a rape can only be proven if there are four male witnesses who come forward to testify. Because this standard of proof is nearly impossible to meet, women who have been raped find themselves likely to be prosecuted for adultery when they give birth to children out of wedlock, even if they have filed charges for rape. In two instances, women were sentenced to jail and public whipping for adultery. One of the women was a house servant who was nearly blind. The positive changes in the Hudood Ordinances include such tepid measures as setting a 10 percent quota for women in government positions. The point to be emphasized here is that these are organized federal structures that limit women's freedom and provide systemic protection to men who inflict violence or rape upon women.

This type of organizing and blaming of victims is not limited to India and Pakistan. Among the controversies surrounding the candidacy of former judge Roy Moore in his campaign for the US Senate are demands on the part of his allies that women who accused Mr. Moore of assault should be prosecuted for bringing forward their allegations, as well as statements by Mr. Moore that a twelve-year-old who had been raped should be condemned because of allegations that she had a sexual disease, though if the allegation were true it was not clear whether the girl contracted the disease as a result of rape or consensual sex. It is important to cast our gaze at the United States and other parts of the more developed world to avoid the error of thinking that these problems are limited to less developed nations. But now we return to Pakistan.

The Punjabi law concerning violence against women arose in the context of significant evidence that such violence takes place routinely ("Women's Protection Bill"). The Wikipedia discussion of domestic violence in Pakistan cites a Human Rights Watch study in 2009 that estimated that somewhere between 60 and 97 percent of women in Pakistan experienced some form of domestic violence, whether by forced sex or beatings ("Domestic Violence in Pakistan"). An essay on violence against women in Pakistan by Lizzie Dardeen, published in the *Independent*, described how men expected to "thrash" their wives occasionally and also listed statistics on honor killings, domestic violence, and other attacks on women (Dardeen, "'Rampant' Violence"). As of 2016, there was still organized resistance to the passage of the Punjabi Women's Protection Bill introduced in 2006, with concern on the part of religious leaders that changes in the laws concerning rape and penalties for domestic abuse of women would lead to an era of free sex ("Pakistan Religious Leaders"). Underlying these views is, of course, the belief that women are the problem that must be controlled, that it is women who are sexually ravenous and out of control, not men.

Pakistan also has a third, informal judicial system that works against the interests of women. When there are family disputes over young men and women meeting each other, or becoming close in ways that do not have prior family approval, local courts of male community leaders mete out judgments and punishments. One case was reported in the *Guardian* in which a local court sentenced a young woman to walk naked through the streets of her town as punishment for her brother's extra-marital affair (Rasmussen and Janjua, "Pakistani Police Arrest Men"). The sister had committed no crime at all, but she was chosen to bear the punishment for her brother and for her entire family.

When a culture so strongly inculcates such a system of values, or of permissions to men to attack women without fear of reprisals, one would expect that some of those cultural forces would continue into the nation's diaspora. The British Cabinet published a report on disparities among the lives of British citizens and residents, based on their ethnicity (Nelson, "UK's Conservative Government"). Early information about the report stated that Pakistani women in England are living in an "entirely different society" and are "shockingly badly integrated," according to multiple news reports, including one by Shari Miller in the *Daily Mail* (Miller, "Pakistani Women"). It is difficult to tease out gender in the statistics of the British government website dedicated to this information, "Ethnicity Facts and Figures," which was begun in October 2017. Roughly half of the Pakistani and Bengali people in the United Kingdom are born there; they tend to have significantly lower levels of employment and income. (Curiously, all the British minority populations have higher rates of post high-school education than the white population.)

In Pakistan itself, women tend to drop out of school because they are viewed primarily as household workers and bearers of children. In England, Pakistani women who do not speak English are common, and it is this group that is said to be living in a "different society." The force of Pakistani cultural structures on women—and men as well—can also be measured by reports on marriage within the community.

Natalie Corner, writing for the *Daily Mail*, cites reports that estimate that 55 percent of British Pakistani women are marrying cousins (Corner, "Young British Pakistani Women"; Lefort, "700 Children Born"). While the *Daily Mail* is not a highly respected British paper, because it has been credibly accused of both racism and far-right viewpoints, other sources have carried similar reports about the basic facts of the lives of Pakistanis in Britain. Steven Swinford, writing in the *Telegraph*, cites comments by Baroness Flather, the first Asian peer and a Pakistan-born woman, concerning cousin marriages and the "appalling disabilities among children" ("First Cousin Marriages"). To be fair, this means that the same percentage of Pakistani or Pakistani-British men are marrying cousins, so the burden of the social pressure rests equally on both genders, though the punishments for noncompliance no doubt weigh more heavily on the women, who may be subjected to honor killings or mutilations if they attempt to marry without family approval. Often these marriages are arranged with cousins either in Pakistan or in the United Kingdom. Ms. Corner reports that, as a consequence of this social system, while British Pakistanis are "responsible for three percent of all births [in the UK], they accounted for thirty percent of British children born with a genetic illness." She reports, further, that according to one agency that studies childhood deaths in Britain, 20 percent of the child deaths in East London, a largely immigrant area, are due to parents being related (Corner, "Young British Pakistani Women"). From the standpoint of the United Nations criteria for genocide, this constitutes a kind of self-imposed community genocide, in the sense that the social structures lead to circumstances in which family lines are imperiled. The British press carries many stories about Pakistani families struggling with children who have autism as well as other disorders.

The Human Rights Watch report on 2016 describes a situation in Afghanistan that is broadly similar to that in Pakistan ("Afghanistan: Events of 2016"). A law to improve women's rights is stalled in the parliament because representatives object to many of its provisions. The legal system provides almost no protection to women who run from abusive relationships. Domestic violence is widely prevalent, and the courts have recently reduced the sentences of men involved in gang rapes and murders of women.

The cultural values of Afghani men also follow them into refugee camps and into their settlement in Western nations. Cheryl Benard, writing for the *National Interest*, comments that "I've worked with refugees for decades. Europe's Afghan crime wave is mind-boggling" (Benard, "I've Worked with Refugees"). Indeed, a search of the web turns up large numbers of documented cases of Afghan men, either alone or in groups, attacking women in Germany and Austria. Heather Timmons, interviewing psychologist David Lisak, asked about the dynamics of these attacks (Timmons, "Groups of Men"). Lisak's response emphasized that the attacks probably begin with an ideology of hating women, just like groups who hate Jews or gays. The refugees also feel dispossessed and weak because of their lack of jobs, status, and resources, and they are angry that these women have what they do not. Then comes a moment when a group decides "let's get one," and they attack. Sometimes the attacks are planned; sometimes they are spontaneous. While this problem of attacks on European women is strongly correlated with Afghan male refugees in particular, it is not limited to that group. Yonas Gebreiyosus has published a book about the assaults on women in African refugee camps, specifically documenting cases in a camp in northern Ethiopia (Gebreiyosus, *Women in African Refugee Camps*). The *Guardian* carried a similar story in 2017 about conditions in a refugee camp in Dunkirk, where women and children were abused, raped, beaten, and trafficked, and where women were sometimes forced to trade sexual favors for basic necessities such as blankets (Townsend, "Women and Children"). A UN High Commission on Refugees report explains how, in some camps, older women have organized to serve as senior mothers or protectors of other women and of children, and how communities of women work together to prevent rape (Ntwari, "UNHCR, Refugees Work Together"). It is important to note, given that the rubric of this section is the organization of attacks on women, that the camps are organized centers of rape. Yes, the camps exist to protect refugees, but at the same time, it is understood that the way they are set up allows patterns of rape and other forms of abuse. No doubt it would be difficult to create separate camps for women and children, or for families, or to exclude individuals who are predators. The point is that the way the current system operates, however well-meaning it may be, it participates in a larger system of organized structures that make it possible for the abuse of women to continue. Aditya Gautam's review of the literature on men who rape, published in the *Times of India*, points to all the factors listed here.

It is easy to look toward Asia and condemn relatively well-known problems in Afghanistan, and even China. Two additional examples of organized structures designed to reduce the safety of women should serve to make the point that this kind of organization for genocide is widespread if not universal. Jina Moore wrote an essay for *Buzzfeed* titled "This Is What Happens to Women's Rights When the Far Right Takes Over." Her subject was the rise of the new rightist government in Poland, where the government is working hard to change laws on contraception in order to eliminate access to the pill. The government is also rolling back provisions for abortion in this largely Catholic country where access to abortion has already been difficult, even for women with demonstrable illnesses or genetically disabled fetuses. Additionally, Poland's government is working to cut the funding of nonprofit agencies that provide shelters and healing services to women who have escaped from homes where they were being physically abused. The rationale provided by the legislators is bizarre. To provide shelters for battered women is a form of discrimination, it has been argued, because there is not an equal provision to provide shelters for men. If there could not be a separate set of facilities for men, the government suggested that men should be permitted to enter women's shelters. The fact that there are few Polish men who run from homes because of domestic violence seemed not to matter. Neither did the fact that the presence of men in battered women's shelters runs against the very principles of safety on which those shelters are designed. As in Asia, Poland also has its notable cases of hypocritical prosecution of rape victims. The essay in *Buzzfeed* relates the story of a fourteen-year-old rape survivor whose case was challenged, after which she was investigated with the potential of being herself charged with the crime of having underage sex.

Of course, there are also cultures where men are raped and kept as sexual slaves, though this practice does not appear to be anywhere nearly as widespread as the rape and sexual enslavement of women and girls. In recent history, one of the more notable examples of boy sexual slavery has been revealed by reports on Afghan soldiers keeping boys in this way, sometimes chained to beds. The practice is long-standing and is called *Bacha Bazi*, which means "boy play," as reported in many sources, including a *New York Times* story by Joseph Goldstein (Goldstein, "Soldiers Told to Ignore Sexual Abuse"). Coalition forces have been advised not to question or to interfere with this long-standing practice of their Afghan allies.

It should be no surprise that the same trend to reduce care for abused women can be seen in the actions of the current American government. *Huffington Post* reported that, under the proposed 2017 Trump Administration Budget, there would be an 18 percent cut to the funding for the Department of Health and Human Services and a 4 percent cut to the budget of the Department of Justice (Jetsen, "Trump's Budget"). These cuts, it was projected by experts, would probably cut services to 260,000 victims of domestic violence in the United States each year. Without shelters and other care, these women and children are likely to be victimized again. This budgetary choice, if it is implemented, organizes or puts into place the conditions for abuse.

Polarization

Sandra Bern's foundational work on polarization points out the myriad ways that the genders are polarized (Bern, "Gender Polarization"). Virtually any difference is exaggerated, and differences are created where there were none. Clothing, hair styles, occupations, social and family roles, professions, and the buttoning of clothing—the polarization is so extreme that it feels both natural and invisible. As a kind of proxy for the problem, one can simply look at the dates when women were allowed to vote in the world, understanding that there are still nations where women cannot vote, as well as at least one, Brunei, where men also cannot vote for anything. It's pointless to look backward at such landmarks as the first female doctor, or admissions to universities, or admission before the bar, when the voting data shows the extent and depth of polarization.

Women were first allowed to vote in national elections in New Zealand, in the modern era, and that change took place in 1893. Here are some others:

- The United States of America, 1920
- The United Kingdom, 1928
- Spain, 1931
- Brazil, 1932
- France, 1945—Yes, not until the end of World War II
- Italy, 1945
- India, 1947, upon independence from Britain
- Belgium, 1948
- China, 1949, upon the new Communist state
- Greece, 1952—home of democracy?
- Mexico, 1953
- Peru, 1955
- Egypt, 1956
- Lebanon, 1957
- Paraguay, 1961
- Monaco, 1962
- Switzerland, 1971
- Portugal, 1976
- Liechtenstein, 1984
- Qatar, 1999
- Oman, 2003
- Saudi Arabia (in municipal elections only), 2015

And then there are nations where the franchise was extended only to be withdrawn: Kuwait and Afghanistan. And nations where there is no female vote: the Vatican ("Timeline of Women's Suffrage").

Another useful index for pondering the degree of gender polarization in the world is the one published by the World Economic Forum. The Global Gender Gap Report for 2016 includes complex indices of four factors: economic participation, education, health, and political participation. The data used for the report are drawn from many international reports and data sets, and the weighting and methodology of the report are explained in detail in the organization's website. For 2016, sufficient data was available to prepare rankings of 142 nations. That year was one of mixed results, with as many nations making progress on the gender gap as those that backslid. Overall, the gap between female and male outcomes on the four scales could be described in this way: Women had 96 percent of what men achieved in health care. Women had 95 percent of male achievement in education. Women managed to get 59 percent of what men had by way of economic participation. And women overall had 23 percent of the political power exercised by men.

Because men and women were compared within each nation, it is possible for a nation to rank fairly high overall even if the levels of attainment are generally low. The analysis looks for differences between what men and women get in a given nation. Consequently, Rwanda, which has manifold problems of war, ethnic violence, sexual violence, and AIDS, ranks fifth among all nations because men and women fare roughly the same. They are not doing well, yet they are sinking in the same boat. Nations can have fairly high female political participation without being very safe. Burundi and South Africa rank twelfth and fifteenth overall in the ranking of women's political power, though they are known for high levels of violence against women (World Economic Forum, "Global Gender Gap Report").

What the Global Gender Gap Report does allow a reader to tease out are the kinds of polarization that exist and how that polarization affects individual scores and overall international ranking. The United States, for example, ranks forty-fifth overall among the world's nations. While there is no perceivable difference in educational attainment or access for American men and women, the women's health score is somewhat low, indicating a difference in the health care received. More telling, the United States ranks twenty-sixth in economic participation by women and seventy-third in female political participation, having the same score on this item as the

People's Republic of China. The global averages, however, are worth repeating. In 2016, women had 59 percent economic participation compared to men and 23 percent political participation compared to men. Note that these figures are the same as for the United States of America, which places it halfway down the ranking of the world's nations in terms of these indices for the polarization of men and women.

In the United States, the Equal Rights Amendment to the Constitution was introduced in 1923, passed by Congress in 1972, and ratified by thirty-eight states. Three more states need to ratify the amendment. Those that have failed to do so include Utah, Arizona, Illinois, Missouri, Oklahoma, and the southeastern United States, including Virginia. The amendment has three brief sections. Section One reads: "Equality of rights under the law shall not be denied or abridged by the United States or by any state on account of sex." Section Two authorizes Congress to enforce the amendment. Section Three says the amendment will take effect two years after it is ratified by the necessary number of states. It must be a polarized nation indeed where such a mild statement of equality cannot be affirmed by every jurisdiction (ERA, "Equal Rights Amendment").

Preparation

According to Gregory Stanton's explanation of genocide, preparation includes defining the victims, making lists, transporting victims, and concentrating them where they can be killed or subjected to other genocidal actions (Stanton, "8 Stages of Genocide"). These are activities focused on the victims themselves. Certainly, preparation must also include a continuation of the activities that Stanton lists under organization. People must be trained and motivated to become killers or abusers. The case of students at a school in Burundi serves as an example of early preparation. As the two thousand male students stand in line in a video, they chant the acts of violence and sexual predation they propose to inflict on women. The video led to international condemnation in view of the carnage that has taken place repeatedly in Burundi, Rwanda, the Congo, and Uganda as parts of the ongoing World War of Africa (Peralta, "U.N. Condemns 'Grotesque Rape Chants'"). One need not turn one's eyes to Africa, however, to see this kind of training take place on an annual basis. Recent reports out of British universities, for example, decry rituals imposed upon "freshers," or what Americans call freshman students. Eleanor Doughty wrote about the "lad culture" at the London School of Economics, where new students were urged to sing a ditty identical to one reported at the University of Nottingham, where new students sang about raping women to death, closing with the line, "now she's dead, but not forgotten, dig her up and fuck her rotten," in the Student Union building (Doughty, "Lad Culture at University"). Jesus College, Cambridge, and Baxter College in New South Wales, Australia, have been the subject of similar reports in recent years (Pearce, "UNSW Is Investigating"; Dawson, "Cambridge Footballers Punished"). Either one views this as "lads will be lads" who after all read "lads' magazines," or one chooses to see the obvious link to the epidemic of campus rapes. The same kind of rough "humor" or preparation for violence is obvious in sports. David Mooney in *The New Statesman* reported on the way that British football players chanted "get your tits out" to a female physiotherapist who was caring for them (Mooney, "Chilling Reality of Sexism"). These activities are not merely individual preparation to abuse women, but they constitute group preparation for serial rapes or gang rapes.

The American university and sports scenes provide many similar examples of systematic preparation for sexual violence, and in view of the seriousness of the problem of rape on American college campuses, one might think that stories about preparation for attacks in the United States would garner as much international opprobrium as what took place in Burundi. Jake New, in a piece for the website *Inside Higher Ed*, reviewed the most recent surveys of schools and concluded that there is no strong evidence suggesting the problem of rape on campus is either better or worse depending either on the size of the school or whether it is private or public (New, "Updated: Sex Assaults"). Liz Anderson, writing a review of the literature for *The Daily Texan*, the University of Texas student paper, explored the connection between organized fraternities and rape. National studies, she wrote, show that fraternity members are three times more likely to rape. Less than 3 percent of students belong to fraternities, though fraternity "brothers" are responsible for over 50 percent of gang rapes. The preparation for gang rapes is complex and thorough. Parties are organized. The male fraternities have the alcohol, and 75 percent of sexual assaults are related to alcohol. Anderson wrote that at the University of Texas, 84 percent of rapes are associated with alcohol. A study reported in *Inside Higher Education* states that 86 percent of frat men engage in binge drinking, compared to 45 percent of men who are not members of fraternities. Students are "listed" for rape in this way: women who appear at some fraternity doors are graded on a ten-point scale. Only those who score six or more are invited in to the parties. Surveys of frat members showed that they have "higher levels of comfort with female pain." The women are transported to the parties or invited to transport themselves to the location, where some of them will eventually be assaulted.

There are also rituals to prepare the men to disrespect women and to be ready to rape. At Yale University, one fraternity was suspended for five years after the members were heard chanting "no means yes, yes means anal" (Foundation for Individual Rights in Education, "Yale University: Fraternity Suspended"). Users on Greekchat.com have posted chants in which members sang about public masturbation, rape, and forcing sex on one hundred women at a time ("Sigma Chi Chants"), while one widely re-ported story from the University of Central Florida concerns a fraternity where a member outside the building chanted "let's rape some sluts." A uni-versity disciplinary panel famously found that the video of this chant broke no university rules (Russon, "Panel Finds Frat"). At another university, however, as reported by Emily Jashinsky, a university dismissed a rugby team for chanting a long poem that began with "found a whore" and ended with a description of how the rapists suffered from sore penises (Jashinsky, "University Dismisses Rugby Team"). Obviously, there is a causal connec-tion between this kind of preparation, this kind of building of expectations, and the reality of campus rapes that will be anatomized later in this book.

Elaine Replogle, a sociologist at the University of Oregon, speculated about the functions of gang rape when analyzing a terrible gang rape in India, where a group of men in a bus turned on a courting couple, accused them of misbehavior for being out together late at night, and ended up shoving an iron rod into the woman's vagina after raping her and then killing her boyfriend. The four men involved were eventually sentenced to death, while the one adolescent received a long prison term (Replogle, personal communication). Replogle's suggestion is that gang rapes of this kind are social activities designed to keep women as a group in their place. This is terrorism in the way that lynching is terrorism with a well-designed purpose. By inflicting monumental and well-publicized harm on a small number of victims, it is possible to terrorize the entire targeted class of people into compliance (Replogle, "Psychology of Gang Rape"). This kind of strategic violence is similar in function to other activities carried out by men to challenge women's freedom, particularly in conservative Muslim nations. Aicha Lemsine, for example, writes about the "agony" of women in Algeria, where gangs of men impose their own understanding of Islamic law, forbidding women to make use of the women's bath houses and imposing other rules on dress and public appearances in the same way that religious authorities patrol in Saudi Arabia. The offenders who commit gang rapes have in some ways been prepared to carry out what they do (Lemsine, "Breaking the Silence"). Aditya Gautam's review of the literature reaches similar conclusions, particularly by pointing to the way that there can be an assumption in India that if a young woman is out late at night, whether accompanied by a male or not, she is violating a moral standard and deserves to be raped as punishment for that violation (Gautam, "Why Do Men Rape").

More fundamentally, there is the question of how heterosexuality has been defined and how its definition has changed. Brendan Ambrosino wrote an essay for BBC on the "invention of heterosexuality" that noted how in the late nineteenth century, when the term was invented, it was used to describe people who had a fixation on sex with the opposite sex, as in having an obsessive, unnatural, and perverse need for sex. Over the course of a century, the definition changed to a description of "normal" sexuality, until that was challenged by various gay rights movements. At the same time, as a glance at any newsstand will indicate, there developed an emphasis on "getting enough," on counting sexual experiences as well as the idea that more is always better. There is, therefore, a sense in which the media in the last century have built an expectation of more sexual activity, and this, too, constitutes a form of preparing both men and women (Ambrosino, "Invention of Heterosexuality").

Altogether, there is abundant evidence that men around the world participate in group activities that prepare them to assault women and teach them rationalizations for that behavior. If one reasonably objects that the examples here have been drawn from a few cultures in Europe, America, Australia, Asia and Africa, I will say again what I said at the opening of this book: We are in a new age of reading and writing. The reader is free to check multiple sources and of course should do so. Evidence presented here suggests that the phenomenon of preparing to harm women is global.

The final stages, genocide itself and denial, follow naturally from all of this careful, steady, well-reinforced preparation.

chapter three

PORNOGRAPHY
AND GENOCIDE

Pornography and Genocide: A Review of the Balkans Case

WHILE THE OBJECT OF this book is to make the case that women always live under conditions approaching genocide, and the most recent evidence is the best indicator that this state of affairs is continuing, the works of Catharine MacKinnon, Celine Bardet, and others must be recognized for their pioneering success in pointing out the issues and doing the very hard work of bringing the Serbian genocide through the complex processes required to make cases before the international criminal courts. Professor MacKinnon is a lawyer, and I am not. Her work with Andrea Dworkin led to the drafting of a controversial and still-foundational ordinance against pornography, and she continues to work to bring cases to the courts and to define the issues in a way that will lead to legal action. This present book has a different purpose: to make a basic case that women are always and everywhere living in a condition where they are imperiled by the presence of multiple genocidal forces, if they are not experiencing genocide itself or the denial that tends to follow genocide. The story of what MacKinnon and others did about pornography and genocide in the Balkans needs to be mentioned and honored because it provides the critical context for understanding everything else in this volume.

One truth that emerges from reading about the work of MacKinnon and Bardet is this: it is possible to commit a crime in a moment that will take decades to unravel and bring to justice. A related truth is still more sobering: we do not live long enough to repair the ill that we do. Cycles of vengeance go on for centuries, if not millennia. This is why it is critical to face the conditions that we have collectively created and to do what we can to bring an end to the evil that is misogyny in all of its forms.

Celine Bardet served in Brčko, Bosnia as the legal officer for the UN Office of Human Rights. Her account of her work there, published as *Zones Sensibles: Une femme en lutte contre les criminels de guerre*, describes not only the crimes, but also the extreme difficulty of addressing genocide. Her work in Brčko required her to mediate a legal system in which new laws were being written to bring war criminals to justice, and in which the legal system itself was transitioning from a French to an American model, which in turn meant an adjustment of thinking about who prosecuted, who investigated, who interviewed, and every other detail of how investigations were carried out and how courts concluded their work. In addition, in a multi-ethnic city, people had myriads of reasons not to testify. Ms. Bardet worked not only with victims of rape whose families had been slaughtered, but also with killers. Some of her accounts are reminiscent of Frantz Fanon's *The Wretched of the Earth*, particularly where Fanon recounts working as a psychiatrist with French soldiers who tortured Algerians and who themselves suffered continuing PTSD, including hearing screams when they went to bed at night and anytime they were alone.

Brčko was the location of the Luka concentration camp, where some three thousand Bosnian Muslims and a small number of Serbs were killed in assembly-line fashion. Victims had their throats cut over a specific drain that swallowed their blood; industrial furnaces were employed to burn the bodies; some victims were set aside for torture, following which they were left to bleed to death or were shot and killed if they had not died in a few days.

A number of familiar themes emerge in her work. First, the international jurists debated whether what was taking place in Bosnia fit the definitions of genocide because the killings could be interpreted as fighting over land and were complex because, in some areas, groups who killed each other in other territories collaborated in this area. The question seemed to be this: Does a finding of genocide require evidence of deliberate intent to target a religious or ethnic group, as compared to simply killing large numbers of people who occupy an area without explicitly stating any religious or nationalist motivation? Specifically, Milorad Dudek, the Prime Minister of the Serbian Republic of Bosnia in 2009, claimed that there could be no genocide because women and children had been spared, even though boys and men had been slaughtered in huge groups by death squads that worked virtually from dawn to dusk. These issues are reminiscent of the current problem in American law of deciding whether there is racial prejudice in the system of justice, an assertion that appears to be true based on the statistical data concerning indictments, convictions, lengths of sentences, and numbers of minorities in prison. Is it in fact necessary to acquire from each police officer, judge, and jury member a declaration of prejudice?

Second, in Bosnia and elsewhere, there was and continues to be a conversation about whether there is a sufficient and substantial difference between findings of crimes against humanity as compared to genocide. The key difference is "intent to destroy." The US State Department has recently struggled with this question in relation to the mass killings of Muslims in the Rohingya area of Myanmar, according to one source (Abdelaziz, "It Would Be Good"). A third theme that emerges from Bardet's work is that there was widespread denial because people continued to live in the same neighborhoods with those who had tortured and killed their relatives after peace was established. There was little safety to speak. Fourth, while men and boys were routinely executed in large groups, women were raped rather than killed. This treatment of women reinforces the case for treating rape as a form of genocide: it is often the preferred form of genocide for women. There was also a commitment to *omerta*, or to complete silence about children born as a consequence of these rapes. Under such circumstances, it was of course difficult for anyone to bring charges for rape, murder, or any other crime because such charges would endanger both the mothers and the children.

Celine Bardet's book is framed by the story of one Bosnian woman, Cvijeta, who was repeatedly raped and who finally was willing to break the code of *omerta* and help to bring her rapists to justice. It took months of sharing coffee and family stories before Cvijeta was prepared to talk about what had happened. Then she required guarantees of safety, followed by yet more months of careful forensic work to discover the identities of those who had assaulted her. Cvijeta asked to see the courtroom where she would testify before she was willing to go to trial. Each of these details reveals the complexity and the enormity of the task of prosecuting even a single case of rape in a way that is sensitive to the fears of the victim and thorough and just in terms of identifying and appropriately prosecuting the offenders.

Yet, as Bardet herself emphasizes, this was just one case of thousands, if not tens or hundreds of thousands.

When Bardet finally left her post with the United Nations, it was still not clear whether there would be successful prosecutions of the genocide that took place in one of the primary death camps. Just as important, the state of war was continuing even though active fighting in the streets had come to an end under the supervision of United Nations and other forces. Neighbors wrote warnings and threats on each other's doors. People were shamed or denied housing or employment because of their past status or deeds. The ethnic divisions persisted. Worse, the trafficking of women that had taken place during the war continued, with truckloads of young women sent off to other nations to work in brothels. That part of the genocide, the rape and trafficking and prostitution, lasted far longer than the organized killing of men and boys. Pakistani UN forces, for example, were sent away for engaging in sexual trafficking. There was also widespread international trading in the organs of people who had been killed. During the genocide itself, there were occasions where people were forced to eat portions of their dead children. Once the limits were off, there was no end to the savagery.

Bardet mentions that Serbs made films when they killed Bosnian Muslims and that those films were sometimes shown on local networks, including B92, the primary Serbian television network. There is a significant discussion on the web about what is called the pornography of war as opposed to sexual pornography. Watching real killing qualifies as a form of pornography to the extent that we experience schadenfreude or other stimuli from immersing ourselves in violence, as we do with a large proportion of what is dished out by the visual media as evening entertainment. During the Vietnam War and since, there have been many battlefield reports that include photos of the dead, if not of the actual killing of people. What Bardet noted was somewhat different again from mere battlefield footage, because the footage was films of soldiers killing civilians as ethnic cleansing, as deliberate genocide. In her book about her service, she does not explicitly mention pornographic films, the filming of Bosnian women being raped. That atrocity was and is the focus of the work of Catharine MacKinnon.

I do not have experience on the ground or in the courtroom; my training is historical, literary, and philosophical rather than legal. However, here I do attempt to generalize, to universalize a point that emerges from the work of Bardet, MacKinnon, and others. My point is to make the case that the genocidal war against women is systemic and global in terms of Stanton's criteria for genocide. It crossed my mind to call MacKinnon's 1993 article in *Ms. Magazine* seminal, though the implied metaphor then shocked me. To inseminate is to plant a seed, and it can also be an act of rape; additionally, it suggests that the trough that receives the seed is merely a convenient space, not a contributor to the growth and nature of what grows. The metaphor is another way to deny, in many cases, the role of the female. Ms. MacKinnon's article is still fruitful because it continues to be reprinted, excerpted, cited, and headlined as the issues she identified continue to surface across the world. Her work in Bosnia and Herzegovina outed the use of pornography in the systematic and widespread use of rape as a part of the genocide carried out by Serbian forces. She explained the "rape theater" created in death camps where women were raped and filmed in the presence of groups of soldiers. In some cases, those rapes were then shown on the Serbian evening news programs, a fact mentioned as well by Celine Bardet. Yugoslavia, Ms. MacKinnon notes, was a nation awash in pornography before the outbreak of the wars that followed the end of Tito's regime. If the abundance of pornography was not sufficient to stimulate rape and to suggest violent actions to perform, soldiers also passed around manuals about sexual acts and decorated pornographic photographs with diagrams of what they intended to do to their next victims. Often, soldiers would invite friends to come watch them rape. These reports challenge the psyche and limits of imagination in the sense that the rapists were twisted into understanding sexuality, generally an intimate and private act, as something to be performed in public under the critical eye of others. MacKinnon writes, "the world has never seen sex used this consciously, this cynically, this elaborately, this openly, this systematically, with this degree of technological and psychological sophistication, as a means of destroying a whole people" (MacKinnon, "Rape, Genocide, and Women's Rights," 16).

Rape, MacKinnon points out, was not an issue in the Nuremberg trials, even though there was abundant evidence of rape and trafficking of women in World War II; it became an issue in the ICTY, the International Criminal Tribunal for Serious Crimes in the Former Yugoslavia. MacKinnon writes of how the ICTY was perhaps "crawling" toward progress on defining rape as genocide (199). She observes as well that it was a sign of progress that, intellectually speaking, the jurists began to understand that the issue was not merely to understand that rape mattered as a crime, or that genocide was a crime, but further to grasp that rape is a form of genocide (184). She is also painfully aware of the way that other definitions stood between victims and justice: once a war is defined as merely a civil war, what happens in a civil war does not count from the perspective of international laws that concern wars between states. Moreover, she strove to make others understand that sometimes what looks like just a civil war is in fact naked genocide carried out by people who have many weapons against people who have hardly any weapons at all. The Bosnians tried a pacifist approach under the leadership of Ibrahim Rugova. It was not powerfully effective in the face of forces that were not after their territory, or their property, or who had some other military or political objective. (The limits of pacifism are discussed in my *Blessed Are the Pacifists: The Beatitudes and Just War Theory* as well as in many other publications.) Those organized against them wanted the Bosnians obliterated. My point is to generalize the findings of MacKinnon and Bardet. To argue that what happened in Bosnia and what is continuing to happen in South Africa, the Congo, Myanmar, and elsewhere is not an anomaly, but rather the existential reality on the ground. Genocide takes place with relative ease because there is a permanent genocidal war underway against the world's women.

Pornography and Genocide Now

In a review article by D. M. Szymanski entitled "Sexual Objectification of Women: Advances to Theory and Research" in *Counseling Psychologist*, sexual objectification is defined as "when a woman's body or body parts are singled out and separated from her as a person and she is viewed primarily as a physical object of male sexual desire." According to studies reported by Andrea Dworkin and Catharine MacKinnon, 80 percent of published pornography does more than objectify women by focusing on their genitalia—it includes violence against women, and it is abundantly clear that those who "use" pornography want images that include violence as well as objectification. Pornography is 100 percent about turning human beings into objects, and at least 80 percent about inflicting violence on those objectified human beings.

It should be no surprise, therefore, that the tanks of Serbian soldiers were plastered with pornographic images as they went about their work of slaughtering men and boys and capturing, raping, filming, and killing women and girls. According to an *ABC News* report written by Lee Ferran in 2016, the computers captured from jihadists in the Middle East were 80 percent full of pornographic images (Ferran, "Jihadists' Computers '80 Percent' Full"). Among these jihadists were troops who kidnapped and raped Yazidi women and girls. Yazidis are a Muslim group that hold a number of beliefs that differ from most forms of Shiite Islam. In 2015, *Reuters* reported that jihadi imams had issued fatwas, or spiritual rulings, on certain limits on the rape of these women (Landay, "Who Can Rape Female Slaves"). Among these rulings were commands that it was improper for both a father and son to rape the same woman, and that it was improper for one man to rape both a mother and her daughters. While slavery and rape are not permitted within orthodox Islam, these battlefield imams had raised no objection to the enslavement and sexual abuse of women who belong to a religious group some of whose doctrines they reject. Their scruples about who gets to rape whom are bizarre.

The United Nations Office of the High Commissioner for Civil Rights reports that in 62 of 188 nations, child prostitution is a travel objective. One accesses information about child prostitution and sale and sexual trafficking through pornographic websites. Children who are used and trafficked in this way are seriously injured and can be expected to suffer from PTSD, should they survive at all ("Annual Reports to Human Rights Council").

Pornography is not disorganized. It is not a matter of some thousands of insurgents gluing pictures to their stolen tanks. It is an international industry. *Economy Watch* calculated the value of the major pornography industries by nation in 2006 ("Porn Industry"). China led the way with an industry worth $27.4 billion, though pornography is technically illegal in China according to Wikipedia sources; South Korea followed with $25.73 billion, then Japan with $19.98 billion, and the United States with $13.33 billion ("Pornography by Region"). The estimates are difficult to evaluate. *Fight the New Drug* reports a global annual value of $97 billion. This is an industry, though, in which much of the "product" is available free. These figures mean little without some comparative context. The annual value of the US forest products industry is $300 billion, and the annual value of the global cosmetics industry is $400 billion ("U.S. Forest Products Industry"; "Cosmetics Industry"). So, the porn industry generates about a third of the value each year of all the eye shadow, lipstick, face powder, skin care products, soaps, shampoo, deodorants, and oral hygiene products sold in the entire world—and a quarter of the value of all wood products sold globally.

Is there a direct connection between pornography and genocide, between pornography and the ongoing war against women that is equivalent to an ongoing genocidal onslaught of one gender against another? Early in this project, I corresponded briefly with Catharine MacKinnon, a pioneer in this area of inquiry and activism who has faced much hostility from those who believe that a little porn is a healthy adjunct to normal sexual development and life. Like a good lawyer, she raised the question of what would constitute a case of pornography being connected to genocide. Her most famous case involved the Bosnian genocide, where soldiers who carried out the genocide consumed pornography, raped Muslim women, and made pornographic films of these rapes to share with other soldiers and with other audiences. This case eventually made its way to international courts. Some websites now purport to offer pornographic films of the Nigerian girls, the Chibok girls, kidnapped by Boko Haram. Is Boko Haram carrying out genocide, or is it merely attempting to control areas of Nigeria, Cameroon, and other nearby nations to impose its own Islamist viewpoint? The girls who are raped and impregnated are certainly victims of a genocidal campaign, as defined in this book (Committee on the Elimination of Discrimination Against Women, "Concluding Observations").

Anyone skeptical of the claims presented here may see a slippery slope, however, in the movement from the demonstrated full-scale genocide, rapes, and pornographic films of Bosnia to the less-thoroughly documented atrocities carried out by Boko Haram groups in central African nations. All of these cases raise issues of criteria and proof, and they all on the one hand call for an expansion of existing definitions of war and genocide, while on the other hand assert standards of proof that may differ from the kinds of proof expected either by courts of law or by social scientists looking for specific kinds of statistical tests and probabilities. What are the stations along this slope of different kinds of stories of gynecide, femicide, female genocide as it is practiced today, and connections or associations between pornography and those cases of murder, rape, and slavery? One relevant point is that when there is a small (relatively speaking) outbreak of genocidal activity against women, there is reason to consider that outbreak part of a global and continuing pattern. Boko Haram does what ISIS does and what other extremist religious groups do to women. None of these groups exists in a vacuum; they learn from each other and model themselves on each other's behaviors (AFP, "L'Afrique du Sud"; "Afrique du Sud"; Center for Reproductive Rights, "Women's Reproductive Rights"; "Chiffre affolant").

A still less forceful connection between pornography, rape, and geno-cide can be found in the many reports that United Nations Peacekeeping troops in Africa have raped women and been known to spend many hours on and off the trails watching pornography on their cell phones ("Kony Hunters Increasingly Disillusioned"; "Rapport sur le génocide"; Berlinger, "U.N. Peacekeepers Accused"; "Dark Side of Peacekeeping"). These rapes have taken place in the context of genocidal attacks, not by UN troops, but rather by forces that the UN has been attempting to control or defeat for over fifty years. Yet at the same time, to the extent that raping and terror-izing women constitutes a crime of genocide, those UN troops are com-mitting genocide while attempting to prevent genocide by others. The UN's Annual Review in 2016 detailed many cases of what the UK's *Independent* called a longstanding problem of sexual abuse including the sexual abuse of children by United Nations peacekeeping troops (MacLeod, "United Nations").

Dionne Searcey, in an article in the *New York Times* on December 8, 2017, tells a similar story about women who fled from Boko Haram only to be raped by Nigerian Security Forces, who took the girls to camps where they were groomed, showered, used as cooks, and then repeatedly raped rather than returned to their families. Her article estimates about seven thousand women raped by Nigerian forces ("They Fled Boko Haram").

One might argue, first of all, that it is not possible in the case of these crimes to demonstrate absolutely certain causal links between watching porn, making porn, raping, and killing. One could also argue that even if such causal connections are plausible, they become more attenuated or weaker as one examines in turn the cases of Bosnia, Boko Haram, and UN Peacekeeping troops in central Africa. In my previous book, *Cain's Crime*, the same kind of problem of causation and the same issues of defining evidence arose in the context of considering just who could be considered collateral damage, civilian casualties, or noncombatant casualties in the various wars now being fought. Army leaders prefer to keep these numbers small, so the standards they set for including casualties are high. A non-combatant casualty is someone who was in the wrong place at the wrong time and was immediately killed in a strike against a nearby enemy target. Moderate critics of war tend to include people who died in near proximity, either close in location or close in time to the attack. This kind of counting includes those who die of injuries and those who are slightly more distant from a drone or missile attack. More strident critics of war set yet a different standard, in the case of attacks in Iraq pointing to half a million or more noncombatants who died as a direct consequence of acts of war that took out electricity to hospitals, sewage systems, water distribution systems, and other civic infrastructure. These deaths may take place over the course of months or even years.

Hurricanes are another issue followed by the same disputes. Are the dead only those who were killed by falling trees and power lines and buildings, or do they include hospital patients who cannot receive care, the elderly who die in overheated nursing homes, people imperiled by foul water and starvation, and so on? The 2017 case of Puerto Rico will be instructive. Over two months after the hurricanes, power has not reached at least half the commonwealth, which means that people are living or dying without refrigeration, air conditioning, medical appliances, and in many cases without safe drinking water. No doubt there will be significant debate over how many deaths occur, and how many can in some way be attributed to the extra stress created by the hurricanes.

The reader may not wish to cast a wide net, instead wishing to see very direct links between pornography and genocide, causal chains of the kind currently required by the US Supreme Court to show racial bias in the system of justice. Michelle Alexander's *The New Jim Crow* documents that issue exquisitely. There is racial bias when a judge or prosecutor says that he intends to sentence black defendants to death in front of witnesses or writes a note to that effect, but there is no racial bias when mere statistics indicate huge disparities in convictions, longer sentences, death sentences, and percentages of populations in prison. To meet the most demanding criterion, one would need those who kill or rape to write notarized statements to the effect that looking at a particular magazine photo or video directly stimulated a specific rape or murder. Still, it is important to make a case for a more generous set of criteria and a lower standard, if not of proof, at least of the plausibility of a connection between pornography and killing. The key background fact (and it is a fact) to bear in mind is that women as a group are the target of ongoing genocide in many parts of the world. One out of every thirty-five women is likely to be killed simply because she is a woman. Many bodies of evidence suggest, without proving it to the most demanding standards of proof, that pornography encourages or provokes violence against women, some of it lethal violence.

To view these basic realities properly, one needs to step even further back and note that there is no evidence that, across the world, large numbers of male newborns are murdered just for being male. Neither is it the case that there is abundant discussion of women being addicted to viewing violent pornographic material about men. Boys are sexually abused around the world and are the object of a tradition of abuse in Afghanistan, but there is no widespread international concern and data about the deliberate trafficking of boys. Rape statistics are about the rapes of women, with few exceptions, such as what is happening in the prisons of Libya in current years ("Rape Statistics"; Sweetman, *Violence Against Women*; UN Family Rights Caucus, "Pron Pandemic"; Thompson, "Global Supply Chain").

As noted throughout this book, the criteria for genocide present a problem, not only because they exclude women as a group, but also because they can be adjusted to exclude many kinds of injury and death. The Holocaust was certainly an effort to kill all Jews. The recurrent Hutu and Tutsi violence involved killing men, women, and children, and the fact that it was sporadic rather than industrially organized like the Holocaust did not prevent it from being called genocide. These are clear or relatively clear cases of genocide, where every member of a type or race is slated for death. A lesser form of genocide occurs when the men are killed and the women are taken as sexual slaves. This is what happened to some Yazidi women, as well as to women in Bosnia. However, is it not also genocide when smaller groups of women are kidnapped, as in the case of the Nigerian Chibok girls, and when they are raped and forced into marriages of convenience? In that case, it seems that the Boko Haram would carry out their crimes on as large a scale as they could support with troops and resources. The fact that smaller numbers of women have been affected is merely an indication of a lack of forces. Within the Yazidi and Nigerian ethnic communities, the norm is to marry within the group, with perhaps some permissible intermarriage. To rape a woman from such a culture is to forcibly change the pattern of marriage, childbearing and inheritance. This is clearly genocide by the current United Nations definition.

Those who believe that pornography is not dangerous cite many reports. Some theorists, such as Pauline Oosterhoff ("Can Porn Be a Positive"), even believe that global sex educators should work with the pornography industry to produce sex education videos. A good example of the discussion appeared in the *BBC News* on September 26, 2017, in a feature article written by Jessica Brown, who reviewed a number of university studies of the effects of pornography. She reports that a study of pornographic websites indicated that 88 percent of the porn had violent content (Brown, "Is

Porn Harmful"). A study led by Neil Malamuth at UCLA found that "men who are sexually aggressive and consume a lot of aggressive pornography are likely to commit a sexually aggressive act," though Brown concludes that porn itself is not "the cause." Malamuth's research, she says, suggests that "porn can be compared to alcohol, [which] isn't necessarily dangerous, but can be for those who have other risk factors." This curious sentence needs to be unpacked.

Alcohol is dangerous enough that it is illegal to drive while mildly intoxicated. The roads are full of signs about alcohol blood levels and sadly decorated in many places with religious symbols and flowers memorializing those who have died in accidents caused by alcohol. Alcohol requires the presence of other risk factors, of course. Still, alcohol is a cause if not the only cause of driving fatalities. Other causes include a propensity to drink and the problem that people lose their judgment when they are drunk. Pornography may not be the sole cause of sexual assault. Other related causes include every culture in the world where men are trained to view women as sexual objects. The same university study showed that porn can be "addictive." Other researchers concluded that, "while they found that the brains of those with compulsive sexual behavior mirrored that of drug addicts, that doesn't necessarily prove that porn is addictive." One is reminded here of the debates over whether cigarette smoking was dangerous, because, after all, many people smoke without showing any ill effects. Another study, according to Brown, showed that watching porn led to a "seven times increase in casual sex . . . but only for those who are unhappy." Yet another study showed an "increase in hostility to women, but only in men who had low agreeableness." Brown's overall conclusion was that "negative effects depend on the individual watching it," which of course is true of other experiences that might prove dangerous, such as drinking, smoking, exposure to asbestos, exposure to ionizing radiation, exposure to HIV, and so on.

On the one hand, it is important to note the rhetorical framework, which is to report the results while minimizing any conclusions and implicitly demanding a higher standard of proof. On the other hand, one can use these minimized results to create a profile of the circumstances in which pornography may be harmless. Such places would be those where people tended to be happy, where the viewers were not disagreeable people, where the viewers had no sexual compulsions, and where they had no tendencies to sexual aggressiveness. It is perhaps fair to conclude that pornography is therefore safe-ish where there is no civil discord, no war, no strong social forces pressing toward aggression against women, and general happiness. Since most of us can be disagreeable at times, one would also need to find circumstances where everyone present was at peace with everyone in the surroundings. The defenders of pornography will go to any length to exculpate their drug.

There is an annual World Happiness Report that may be helpful here. If one judges that 50 percent of the world's nations are relatively happy and 50 percent relatively unhappy, then for 2017 the following places are not good for watching porn. This World Happiness report does not include every nation every year, so some blessed and some very sad places tend to be left out. The bottom half of the list for 2017 runs as follows: Croatia, Kosovo, China, Pakistan, Indonesia, Venezuela, Montenegro, Morocco, Azerbaijan, Dominican Republic, Greece, Lebanon, Portugal, Bosnia, Honduras, Macedonia, Somalia, Sudan, Vietnam, Nigeria, Tajikistan, Bhutan, Kyrgyzstan, Nepal, Mongolia, South Africa, Tunisia, Palestine, Egypt, Bulgaria, Sierra Leone, Cameroon, Iran, Albania, Bangladesh, Namibia, Kenya, Mozambique, Myanmar, Senegal, Zambia, Iraq, Gabon, Ethiopia, Sri Lanka, Armenia, India, Mauritania, Congo, Georgia, Democratic Republic of Congo, Mali, Ivory Coast, Cambodia, Sudan, Ghana, Ukraine, Uganda, Burkino Faso, Niger, Malawi, Chad, Zimbabwe, Lesotho, Angola, Afghanistan, Botswana, Benin, Madagascar, Haiti, Yemen, South Sudan, Liberia, Guinea, Togo, Rwanda, Syria, Tanzania, Burundi, and the Central African Republic. Some of these nations, of course, are known as centers of mass rape, including South Africa and the Democratic Republic of Congo. This list includes many nations that produce pornography, though some of the major producers—such as South Korea and the United States—are among the happier, as is Thailand and some other centers of sexual trafficking. While presenting this whole list may seem excessive, it serves to make the point that the global problem of pornography, rape, and violence is probably not well modeled by psychological studies of a hundred or so student volunteers at elite universities in California and Sweden, whose reactions were the basis of some of the research reported by Ms. Brown. To this it may be added that even in the relatively happier United States, about 9 percent of men suffer from daily depression, and nearly 31 percent suffer from depression at some time in their lives (American Psychological Association, "By the Numbers"). Sadness, of course, is less severe than clinical depression, and in any case, one can't know how many of the sad and depressed men in America may experience a sevenfold increase in casual sex after viewing pornography. Nor can one predict whether that urge to engage in casual sex pushes those men to violate any of their normal boundaries with respect to force, consent, prostitution, or trafficking.

Yet another useful index is the Global Safety and Crime Index, in which each nation has a total score of a hundred that consists of the sum of its Safety and Crime indices. For 2017, Venezuela is the nation with the highest risk of crime, followed by South Africa, Papua-New Guinea, Honduras, and Trinidad and Tobago. The United States ranks forty-fourth, and the United Kingdom sixtieth in danger from crime out of 110 ranked nations ("Crime Index for Country 2017"). The Democratic Republic of the Congo was not rated in that year's scale. The safest nations, with the last the safest, were Austria, Taiwan, Qatar, and Singapore. South Africa and Trinidad and Tobago, of course, are among the nations with the highest rates of rape. Perhaps it is appropriate to suggest that people should at least not view porn or other media that tend to encourage violence if they live in the half of the world that is less safe.

To return to the spectrum of types of genocide that take the form of gynecide, the United Nations criteria speaks directly to the use of rape to breed children who are ethnically different. Many of the Yazidi women enslaved and raped by ISIS fighters do not wish to care for the children who were the result of those rapes. The children themselves are obviously not to blame, though they may never find a community that will accept them. Still, one understands the dilemma faced by the mothers, which is related to the dilemma that American law makes it legal to abort a child who is the result of a rape. I do not argue for or against abortion here. I merely note that, even in the most restrictive periods of American law, abortion was permitted if the mother's life was in danger or if the child was the product of a rape. In other words, being raped was a kind of threat of death to which a proper self-defense was to kill the fetus. Or, perhaps being a child of rape meant that one was not human and therefore disposable. Further, perhaps the American law, like the customs of other nations, recognized that the child of a rape was not likely to be accepted anywhere. On the other hand, one of the curiosities of world law is that, in many nations, a defense against being punished for rape was to marry the woman you had raped. More on this tradition later.

Another way to look at the condition of the Yazidi women, who stand as proxies for tens of thousands or more women worldwide at any time, is to focus in a different way on the meaning of death. Family members reported that some of these Yazidi girls and women, when they were returned to their families, were in nearly catatonic states. They did not merely reject the children that had been forced upon them by rape, but also their family members and food. They wanted to sleep and hide themselves. They had been raised, of course, to view rape, extramarital sex, and childbearing as deeply shameful acts, acts that in many of the surrounding cultures would be grounds for family "honor" killings. Does their state constitute a kind of death? Extermination and genocide normally refer to killing bodies. Is it reasonable to extend the idea of genocide to what might be called killing souls (or psyches)? Leonard Shengold, who has written extensively on this topic, traces the concept of soul murder to Strindberg, Ibsen, and one of Freud's cases (Shengold, *Soul Murder*). Extreme child abuse leaves permanent marks; in the case of the Yazidi women who have been captured and enslaved, raped, and perhaps shared around, and have borne the children of their rapists, their states of continuing shock constitute soul murder. Under the circumstances of their future lives in Iraq and elsewhere, it is unlikely that the resources and expertise will be available either to "treat" the deaths of their souls (or psyches) or to research the trajectories of their misery as they age. My aim is not to introduce definitions that are sloppy or overbroad, but rather to open the inquiry to real phenomena that are permanently disabling, though short of physical death. In this case, both the UN criteria for genocide and a concept used broadly in contemporary psychology and psychiatry agree that there can be murder of the soul as well as murder of the body, with effects that are similarly permanent. Recent Swedish studies of Yazidi refugees have led to a newly defined condition: resignation syndrome. Those who suffer from this syndrome lose their desire to do anything but lie in bed (Sallin, "Resignation Syndrome"; Pressly, "Resignation Syndrome"; Callimachi, "Freed from ISIS").

For the record, the literature on resignation syndrome makes two general observations. First, while it is curious that the syndrome has been reported and studied only in Sweden, where it was defined, that does not indicate that the condition is limited to Sweden. Second, many articles in the medical literature, including those by Thomas, Sallin, and others, argue that resignation syndrome is merely another name for a well-known phenomenon: psychogenic catatonia (Sallin, "Resignation Syndrome"; Pressly, "Resignation Syndrome"; Callimachi, "Freed from ISIS"). Cases reported in recent press coverage of survivors of Libyan prisons describe similar symptoms, such as a complete loss of will to do anything and lying all day in bed in a fetal position.

Yet a different, perhaps more existential case is posed by the murder of Abdeer Qassim al-Janabi, a fourteen-year-old Afghan girl raped, stabbed, and murdered by a group of American soldiers who also killed her father, her mother, and her five-year-old sister (Morgan, "Rape, Murder, and the American GI"). There is no doubt that the US military has a problem with the widespread use of pornography ("Porn in the U.S. Armed Forces"). Without examining this case in depth, one can't say what role pornography played in whetting the sexual appetites of the killers. From the standpoint of associating pornography with genocide, the broad issue here is whether it is appropriate to call the sixteen-years-and-counting American presence in Afghanistan a war of genocide, when the goal is to fight terror, which is sometimes understood to mean radical Islamic fighters or their ideology, in a situation where the occupation of a country produces more radicalized fighters, and where some on both sides view that war as part of a larger clash of civilizations in which everyone is a legitimate target, whether wedding guests hit by a drone's missiles or vacationers in Barcelona or Nice run down by trucks. Stepping back from the immediate carnage, one question might be this: Is the death of Abdeer a case in which a war laid the groundwork for gynecide, or is it rather the case that the overall war is genocidal and aimed at both genders, and the gynecide is just part of an ongoing genocide? The easy answer is to say that it is an exaggeration to suggest that ongoing small-scale terror attacks across the world constitute genocide, because genocide must be localized and big. The harder answer is to say that in some cases, as in the case of the worldwide war against women, genocide and gynecide are activities that, like some diseases, are latent everywhere and break out sporadically (though predictably), with very large numbers of casualties over time. The larger, existential question relates to the way that, once any of the fragile boundaries of civilization are broken, a Pandora's box of horrors runs free that always includes women among the first targets, though children and men of other religions and cultures are also destroyed, and in the case of the Bosnian and Kosovan atrocities, the list of crimes includes not only trafficking truckloads of women into prostitution, but also the harvesting of human organs for transplants in other nations.

What kinds of cases can be put forward in evidence that gynecide is a worldwide problem and that it may be caused by pornography? The United Nations criteria are important here: genocide includes rape and other forms of sexual assault that produce such conditions as PTSD. If the general thesis of this book is correct, that women are always in the middle stages of Gregory Stanton's stages of genocide, then one would expect that whenever the normal moderating forces of what has been called the "social fabric" are loosened, threatened, or weakened, then gynecide is likely to occur (with the exception of those places where gynecide is already part of the normal social fabric, as it is in those nations where female infanticide and bride murder are common, such as China and India [where Amartya Sen's original research indicates that the bulk of gynecide takes places], Pakistan and Bangladesh [to a lesser extent], and another dozen nations).

The social fabric could be weakened by forces that make people unhappy, destabilize government, lead to depression, and create uncertainty. Within the United States, one of the most obvious examples is the case of the millions of college students who, whether they leave home or not, move from early adolescence into adulthood by joining social incubators that radically change much of how they live. They share rooms, live in group housing, eat meals and take classes together, entertain themselves in groups, encounter cultural and racial differences, and face ideas that may challenge or undermine long-held assumptions. College students experience shock, malaise, depression, unhappiness, and strong needs for new affiliations and support groups. Away from the supervision of high school, parents, and other family and community members, they navigate their sexual identities and abandon distasteful and confining rules. Multiple studies (for example, Carr and VanDeusen, "Risk Factors"; Carroll et al., "Generation XXX"; O'Reilly et al., "College Student Attitudes"; Shields and Kane, "Social and Psychological Correlates"; and others) indicate that about 90 percent of college men surveyed use pornography. One study says about 40 percent use pornography one or two times a week. The study by Carroll et al. found that 31 percent of college women used pornography. Shields and Kane's study found that the use of pornography may correlate with higher GPAs, so perhaps pornography is not so bad as others had argued, if one is willing to trade off a correlation with rape and sexual assault for a correlation with higher grades.

However, there also appears to be a significant problem with "revenge porn," which is sending out pornographic pictures of former friends whom you wish to punish. This is not exclusively a college problem. An opinion piece on CNN, written by Amy Adele Hasinoff, stated that 10 percent of American women under the age of thirty, according to one survey, had been the victim of having intimate pictures posted on the web without their permission, whether as revenge or for some other reason.

Ms. Hasinoff says that Facebook could profit from the policy of the "legal US porn industry," which requires models to sign permission forms (Hasinoff, "Policy"). I do not know if this claim is true about the pornography industry in the United States. If there are such forms, then whether or not the participants in the "legal" pornography industry exercise complete freedom to sign is open to discussion. Are these forms notarized? Are they completed in the presence of an authority that can determine whether the signatories are acting without duress? This is a key issue, as one reason for child pornography being illegal is that children are not at an age of consent that would allow them to sign such permissions, forms, or contracts. It would be logical if all women who were used in pornography were also required to sign forms permitting that use, with the signatures acquired in circumstances where it could be shown there was no duress. If not, the pornography would be illegal. Better still, the burden of proof should be placed on pornographers to show that such standards have been met; otherwise what they sell should be banned.

There is a high incidence of rape and sexual assault on college campuses, estimated to range between 10 to 29 percent of all female students, though it is well-known that a large percentage of rapes and assaults are not reported, which leads to estimates of the dark or unknown figures of crime ("Campus Sexual Assault"; "Dark Figure of Crime"). Perhaps the rape statistics on campus were equally high before the Internet and the widespread availability of common pornographic magazines. If that is the case, then pornography may be a smaller factor than all those other destabilizing forces that mobilize aggression and take advantage of the ways in which women are symbolized, objectified, dehumanized, and made ready for attack. In the past, however, colleges tended to have binding rules that separated the genders. The National Sexual Violence Resource Center also reports that about 20 percent of women on campus are raped, though 90 percent never report the attack ("National Sexual Violence Resource Center"). The US Department of Justice also reports between 15 and 20 percent of women on campus are raped, depending on the study referenced, and another 12 percent are victims of attempted rape, for a total of up to 32 percent assaulted (Bureau of Justice Statistics, "Rape and Sexual Assault"). Those who are raped are part of the 89,000 women raped annually in the United States.

Translating those percentages into numbers is not necessarily straightforward. Here is an approximation. The National Center for Educational Statistics says about twenty million students are in college, of whom roughly 60 percent or twelve million are now women. If 20 percent of those women are raped, that means about 240,000 raped. It is impossible to meaningfully compare this figure to any annual figure for rapes, such as the 89,000 American women that the Department of Justice estimates are raped annually. We don't know if the 20 percent of college women who are raped are attacked once in two years of community college, or four years of undergraduate study, or eight or more years of medical or doctoral study. The figure says nothing about whether those women are raped once or gang- or train-raped repeatedly or on many occasions. This crude analysis does not take into consideration whether the estimates include unreported crimes. However the math may work out, the evident fact is that rape is a very large problem, first of all in the United States, which ranks among the top nations for reported or estimated rapes. Moreover, colleges are obviously places where enormous numbers of rapes take place. Most significantly, there is a high correlation between the use of pornography and the occurrence of rape in colleges; though, of course, correlation does not necessarily mean causation. Perhaps those preparatory pornographic chants are more causative.

For comparison, the US Department of Justice provides a list of the nations with the highest rates of rape: Lesotho is at 93 percent, Trinidad and Tobago at 58 percent, Sweden at 53 percent, Korea at 33 percent, New Zealand at 31 percent, the United States at 29 percent, Belgium and Zimbabwe at 26 percent, and the United Kingdom at 23 percent. Canada lags with 1.5 percent (Bureau of Justice Statistics, "Rape and Sexual Assault"). When one reads these figures, it is important to keep in mind the phenomenon of "dark crime," or crimes that go unreported. Several Wikipedia discussions pursue this topic. Based on various methods of analysis, they assert that, in the case of rape, probably 91.6 percent of rapes are not reported. The figures cited from the Department of Justice may take dark crime into consideration, as it is widely understood that rape is a particularly personal and humiliating crime that women decline to report for many reasons in all cultures.

The other side of this equation is, of course, the men who rape. It's very odd how the data on rape is presented in the passive voice. So many women are raped, but someone must do the raping. For the most part, the data do not indicate the percentages of men who rape, how many men rape multiple times, and so forth. So, perhaps the most that can be said with certainty is that American colleges are places with enormous consumption of pornography where some significant proportion of the 40 percent of students who are male engage in rape. How this tradition affects the later development of those men and their later actions is not clear, though it cannot be good for a society. Higher education is one of the primary drivers of social and economic mobility; if it is also a center for rape, then college and its educational opportunities are not entirely safe places to overcome the many ways in which women are forced to live in high stages of the genocide scale.

It follows that if one wishes to look for instances where rape is likely to break out at rates surpassing the usual annual totals, one should look for any signs of public disturbance that might overcome the tenuous control that societies maintain when women live in a world where they are always exposed to higher stages of the genocide scale. For example, Hurricane Katrina in New Orleans produced many true and some false stories about rapes of women taking shelter in the Superdome and elsewhere in the city. The normal mechanisms for reporting rapes were disrupted by the flooding, though a temporary means for reporting rapes received 42 reports, according to an NPR report by John Burnett. The article implied that this was a significant number, because the women who made reports had to figure out a way of doing so with many of the normal policing functions overburdened and with many means of communication disabled. Following several major US hurricanes in 2017, newspapers were full of warnings about the possibility of rape outbreaks, though stories at this time—a few weeks after the hurricanes—have been slow to come in.

Similarly, in the recent battle between the government of Mali, French soldiers, and Islamist insurgents, instances of gang rape have "shocked the nation" (Solomon and Koura, "Gang Rapes in Mali"). Even in the horrible circumstances of the Ebola epidemic in coastal West Africa, *Foreign Policy* reported that teen pregnancy in Sierra Leone was up 65 percent. The journal explained that in circumstances where "football games were canceled and bars were closed," men were "forced into close quarters with women and children." Meanwhile, girls were out of school and isolated at home, and some girls whose families had died traded sex for food. Moreover, in Sierra Leone, which has one of the highest rates of maternal death, teen mothers still have a higher incidence of complications and death, with their babies likely to die as well. Here again rape can sometimes mean a death sentence (Yasmin, "Ebola Rape Epidemic"). In Burundi, in 2017, where there has been ongoing ethnic killing associated with the larger war that has included the Democratic Republic of the Congo, Uganda, and Rwanda, a United Nations group condemned a Burundi youth militia, which was filmed chanting songs that encouraged the members to rape people of other ethnicities in order to make babies of their own kind (Peralta, "U.N. Condemns 'Grotesque Rape Chants'"). This differs little, though, from a report issued by the Southern Poverty Law Center in the United States, which highlighted several cases in the United States of men, following the election of President Trump, yelling out to women that they would now be grabbed by the pussy or raped because Trump was president (Miller and Werner-Winslow, "Ten Days After"). Nor does it differ from the accounts of male college students chanting about how they will disrespect, assault, rape, and despise the women they injure.

India has recently provided an example of how widespread genocide by infanticide may be connected to rape. Rape is the fourth most common crime in India, with nearly 25,000 rapes reported in 2012 and 37,000 in 2014. Shahan Khan, in an article for the *Daily Beast*, pointed out that one cause of rape may be an imbalance in the sex ratio due to infanticide. In Gujarat, the ratio of male to female has dropped to 112 to 100 (Khan, "India's Rape Crisis"). This ratio, however, pales by comparison to one report coming out of Tibet by Michèle Dayras, a French reporter who states that a resurgence of male supremacy in Tibet has led to a gender balance in 2008 of seventy girls to one hundred boys. She also says that there has been a rise in prostitution, with pornography as a contributing factor to the objectification of women that is consistent both with prostitution and with female infanticide (Dayras, "China—Tibet"). This claim is so extreme that it requires further research, though there have certainly been many disturbing reports coming from Tibet in recent years. It is difficult, however, to corroborate the many reports coming from activist organizations that are working for Tibetan independence. These can be found on the Internet by anyone willing to search. Many of the reports claim that the Chinese, in addition to assaults on monasteries and other centers of traditional power, have forced Tibetan women to be sterilized.

A UN report in 2003 listed the following nations where mass rape was taking place, though the report did not emphasize pornography as a causative factor: Bosnia, Cambodia, Liberia, Peru, Somalia, and Uganda

("United Nations Office on Drugs and Crime"). Thirteen years later, *Al Jazeera* reported further on the continuing chaos in Cambodia, citing a report from 2013. Author Aela Callan noted that one out of every five men in Cambodia raped and that "violent pornography or violence in the house has become a manual for young men who have no other good role models." The article argued that this pattern of sexual violence was a consequence of Cambodia's horrific civil war and genocide (Callan, "It's a Man's World"). Donna M. Hughes, a leading scholar in this field, has written extensively about other aspects of the problem of pornography, rape and genocide in Cambodia. In an article titled "Welcome to the Rape Camp: Sexual Exploitation and the Internet in Cambodia," she explains that "Rape Camp" is in fact a website that focuses on violent sex using Cambodian women. The market for prostitution and pornography was expanded by the arrival of 10,000 United Nations troops to help rebuild the nation after the genocide carried out by Pol Pot. Hughes points out that rape is often a death sentence because rape and prostitution lead to AIDS (44). The journal *AIDS Alert* confirmed in 1999 that Cambodia's HIV infection rate was the highest in Asia ("Cambodia's HIV Rate"). Danika Gloege writes, as well, about the way that child soldiers in many conflicts are forced to participate in pornography (Gloege, "Shackles That Enslave").

These reports left out the situation in Liberia, where a long civil war produced an epidemic of rape reported in still other United Nations papers. During that civil war, the United Nations stated that between 61 and 77 percent of all girls and women in Liberia were raped, often gang-raped (Gray, "Liberia").

In many of these instances of rape accompanying civil discord, forces sent to assist become part of the problem. The *Daily Mail* reported, for example, a case in which US contractors abused 54 Columbian girls, while *Fight The New Drug* reported on the porn addiction of US forces in many areas (Daily Mail, "US Soldiers and Contractors"; "Porn in the U.S. Armed Forces"). Catharine MacKinnon's report on UN troops in Bosnia includes examples of UN peacekeeping troops asking women in Zagreb how much they cost. In fact, the Internet provides many official UN reports and news stories about UN troops engaging in the use of pornography, raping and sexually exploiting women, and recruiting children for sex. Aid workers from other agencies have also been reported for sexually abusing women in the Sudan and in refugee camps in Morocco (Khaleeli, "Addressing the Sexual Misconduct"). A French website for the news outlet *le Phare* wrote (my translation) that "If the UN wants proof of war crimes in the Congo, it need look no further than its own troops guilty of sexual slavery, sexual aggression, sex trafficking, prostitution, and pornography involving children." In spite of these horrors, the United Nations has not taken steps to act against pornography itself, though a prohibition of pornography is part of an Optional Protocol for the Convention on the Rights of the Child as of January 2002 (United Nations Treaty Collection, "Optional Protocol"). This recommendation is optional, although the UN Family Rights Caucus on the harms of pornography noted that pornography is big business, porn is addictive, users escalate, the escalation can lead to violence, and 87 percent of child molesters use hardcore porn (UN Family Rights Caucus, "Porn Pandemic").

The police themselves are the rapists in some nations. *Huffington Post* ran a long story about Fartuun Abdisalaam, a Somali woman who charged the local security forces with rape, only to find herself charged with a crime and then imprisoned (Adan, "Somalia's Shocking Response to a Rape Report").

More relevant to the case presented here, perhaps, are those cases in which rape was accompanied by torture and murder. Loulla-Mae Eleftheriou-Smith, reporting for the *Independent*, presented a story of a sixteen-year-old Somali girl who was gang-raped, then stabbed and tortured (Eleftheriou-Smith). News reports from South Africa include an increasing number of cases where gangs not only rape girls, but kill them after inserting bottles and other objects into them, sometimes deliberately breaking the bottles to produce cutting edges inside the victims' bodies. This is as good a place as any to note a fact related by James Ferguson in a book about the dangers of Somalia (Ferguson, *World's Most Dangerous Place*). The problem of pornography starts at the top of insurgent organizations. Osama bin Laden's final hideout in Abbottsford, Pakistan, was full of pornography, though according to reports he also had a collection of Disney movies and interviews with academics such as Noah Chomsky (Moore, "CIA Director Mike Pompeo"). It is hard to know whether porn is most popular in the more liberal West or in the more puritanical Muslim world. An Israeli-based organization claims that, according to Google, the nations that make the most use of porn sites are Pakistan, Egypt, Vietnam, Iran, Morocco, Saudi Arabia, and Turkey, though there are aspects of this site that render it questionable, including misnumbering the rankings, as well as the fact that Vietnam is among the top nations, which is not Muslim ("Selon Google, six pays").

Through 2017, another location where reports of rape and murder have been rife is the Rohingya area of Burma (Abdelaziz, "It Would Be Good"). As one can see, and as the International Justice Report observed in June 2013, "communities affected by genocide often become target areas and possess a concentration of sex trafficking victims" ("International Justice Mission"). The Irish Center for Human Rights reported in 2010 that the Rohingya area was already a center of rape, with thousands of documented cases, where rape was used as a "strategy of war" by Burmese army forces. There, as among the Yazidi, the women who are raped feel "unclean," can be ostracized, and find that rape is often followed by murder. In 2017 the *Irrawaddy* journal reported, as the genocide continued and over half a million fresh refugees sought to cross into Bangladesh, that as early as the 1990s, while there were official laws against porn in Myanmar or Burma, "reports say that possession of pornography or erotic movies became widespread among political and army elites during the late 1990s" (Irrawady, "Murky Waters"). No place was safe. *Religion Today* reported that a grandmother hiding alone in a church was raped and tortured. It is worth noting that in Myanmar, which has moved slowly from a totalitarian state to something of a democracy led by a Nobel Peace Prize winner (who is now controversial), the genocide in question, which involves targeting a large Muslim minority who live along the Bangladesh border, has gone on for decades. The groundwork was well in place in the 1990s, and the killing and rape continue in 2017. As of November 2017, reports of rape and murder were still coming out of the Rohingya area, including one by Salma Abdelaziz for CNN that included a case in which a woman's child was murdered in front of her before she was taken in a house, raped, had her throat slashed, and was left with other women in the house, which the soldiers lit on fire. Somehow, she escaped and recovered sufficiently to relate what had happened (Abdelaziz, "It Would Be Good").

In 2017, Katelyn Fossett, writing for *Foreign Policy*, asked the question, "How does a country develop a sixty percent rape rate?" (Fossett, "How Does a Country Develop"). She referred to a *Lancet Global Health* study of Asian nations that reported that Papua New Guinea had a 59 percent rape rate, based on what "men admitted" to doing as part of a formal scientific survey. One wonders, of course, how many men either declined to admit what they did or fabricated their participation. Papua New Guinea has been the site of a generally underreported civil war, which in the period from 1988 to 1998 produced upwards of 20,000 casualties, though figures vary, and some estimates of ongoing strife in the nation have posted higher figures for a combination of civil war and attacks on rural populations by corporations developing resources.

A reasonable reader might well object that these last paragraphs have primarily demonstrated that rape is a massive global problem. The connection to pornography may seem more tenuous. A review of those same paragraphs shows that pornography is mentioned as a causative or associated factor in most of the circumstances where there are large numbers of rapes, and that there is not always evidence that groups of rapists and murderers film what they do. At the same time, there is overwhelming evidence that the rape of women is a huge global phenomenon, and that the availability of pornography is equally enormous and global to the point that it would be difficult to identify a location where one could perform research on what might transpire where rape was not already a tradition and where pornography was not available. How strong is the overall evidence? What standard of proof is required? At what point is the correlation sufficiently strong to indicate that action is required?

Lest these reports become numbing, the remainder of this chapter will focus on the three rape capitals of the world: South Africa, the Democratic Republic of the Congo, and the emerging information about the rape and filming of men being raped in the ongoing civil conflict in Libya, where the accounts seem to assume that women are raped as a matter of course, while the distinctive part is the organized and prepared serial raping of men to destroy their will or ability to fight, to reduce them to victims of post-traumatic stress disorder or resignation syndrome. In all of these cases, there is evidence of the use of pornography. There is also substantial evidence of the production of pornography as part of assaults.

It was Margot Wallstrom, UN Special Representative on Sexual Violence in Conflict from 2010 to 2012 who called the Congo "the rape capital of the world," though others consider South Africa a contender for the title (Lloyd-Davies, "Eastern DR Congo"; Mulumeoderhwa, "Forced Sex, Rape and Sexual Exploitation"). South Africa is a particularly interesting case because television was first introduced on a limited basis after World War II, according to some sources, only to be banned (Bornman, *Violence in South Africa*; Kenyon, "Effects of Televised Violence"). Television may have become permanently available again as early as 1971, though it was officially permitted on a large basis in 1975, with a formal study of the effects of TV initiated in 1974 to provide a year to study the conditions before television so that the effects of allowing television could be measured. That baseline research led to a number of studies that attempted to track the effects of televised violence on the South African culture. Like most studies of violence on television, those in favor of television found much to criticize, while others found the results disturbing and concluded that there was good reason to believe that the availability of television and its violence increased violence in the society. Those studies raise the same questions raised repeatedly in this book: how is it possible to determine with satisfactory scientific or statistical proof that violence on television promotes violence in life, or that pornography promotes violent sexual excesses in life? This issue has become more charged with the introduction and popularity of violent video games, as indicated by a recent American Psychological Association review article that concludes that children who play such games become "less sensitive to the pain and suffering of others," "more fearful of the world around them," and "more likely to behave in aggressive or harmful ways toward others" ("APA Review Confirms Link"). Blanch Pretorius raised similar concerns about the levels of violence in South African children's television (Pretorius, "South African Children's Television Programmes"). Two of these findings are identical to those reported for male college students who have been prepared to assault women by various traditions passed on at colleges in at least the United States and Britain. UNESCO has also published a survey of media violence (Atal and Kosambi, *Violence Against Women*).

After the end of apartheid, as Teboho Maitse wrote in his essay on political change, rape, and pornography in post-apartheid South Africa, in a collection edited by Caroline Sweetman, there was both a large increase in the availability of pornography and a large increase in rape (Sweetman, *Violence Against Women*). There was also a large increase in gambling, which had been banned under the conservative apartheid regime, and there was a strong feeling on the part of many citizens that it was appropriate to embrace anything that had been condemned by the previous, puritanical government, no matter what the effects on the society. The *New York Times* had a similar report (Keller, "Apartheid's Gone and Anything Goes"). The old South African laws banning pornography were repealed and replaced by a Film and Publication Board (see Film and Publication Board website). Early on, feminist scholars began to look at the results of this social experiment. In particular, Diana Russell analyzed the flow of American pornography into South Africa (Russell, "US Pornography Invades South Africa"). And while a South African Human Sciences Research Panel in 2007 stated that it was difficult to find or develop accurate statistics of the levels of pornography and pornographic images of children in the country, there is an entire section of Eyewitness News, a South African media site, dedicated to listing cases of people arrested or convicted for making and selling child pornography, sometimes in collaboration with international networks (Dawes and Govender, "Use of Children in Pornography"; "Eyewitness News").

The evidence suggests that pornography is directly related to the increase in sexual violence. The comment of Kenneth Meshoe, president of the South African Christian Democratic party, was cited earlier, and testified to a concern in the nation's courts about the number of rapists who stated that they were influenced by pornography ("La Justice Sud Africaine"). Hannah Summers, writing in the *Guardian*, reported at the end of 2017 about a clinic that served children who had been raped, where the counselor found that those rapists, too, were inspired by pornography. According to the piece, one out of every ten South African rape victims is now under the age of ten (Summers, "Fighting Child Sex Crimes"). SAPA's article on the "Sunday Rapist" tells a similar tale, though isolated cases do not, of course, amount to statistical proof. Another similar case was reported by the *Chronicle* in Zimbabwe, where two teenage boys confessed that they raped a classmate by turns, taking their inspiration from pornography they had watched (Ncube, "2 Pupils to Be Caned"). Romi Sigsworth's remarkable pamphlet, "Anyone Can Be a Rapist," offers a detailed consideration of the causes of sexual violence in South Africa, though his analysis notes the influence of alcohol on rapes and does not make any reference to or recommendations concerning the increased availability of pornography in the country. Overall, the picture that emerges is one in which laws against pornography were repealed, American pornography entered the nation in force, many changing social forces led to a highly unstable set of relations among racial and economic groups, and South Africa found itself faced with a crisis of rape and sexual violence.

If it were true that the vicarious violence of television somehow drained off the human tendency to violence, then one would not expect to have seen the increased doses of violence on television, to the point that autopsies and torture are a standard feature of mainstream television series.

Catharine MacKinnon makes this point in *Butterfly Politics* (203), citing many studies. If it were true that vicarious violence drained off our species' tendency to hurt, then there would not be such concern about copycat killings and massacres. This chapter is being written in the days following the mass murder in Las Vegas, Nevada, where a single man with nineteen assault rifles fired into a crowd of as many as twenty or thirty thousand outdoor concert-goers. At this time, the total number of deaths is 59, and the number of injured is 527. No doubt police authorities are working hard to determine whether this massacre will stimulate someone who hopes to exceed these totals. By the second decade of the twenty-first century, Doctors Without Borders estimated, according to a report in *Jeune Afrique*, that a woman was being raped in South Africa every twenty-six seconds, with the chief victims being girls between the ages of twelve and seventeen (AFP, "Afrique du Sud"). *Slate Afrique* estimated in 2015 that there was a reported rape in South Africa every ten minutes ("Chiffre affolant"). *Le Point* published an article that estimated there was a rape in South Africa every seventeen seconds, with 40 percent of women raped sometime in their lifetimes, compared to 3.5 percent of men, which is a staggering figure in itself. According to this source, 25 percent of the rapists had HIV, so that they were likely conveying a potentially fatal disease to their victims. The victims mentioned in the article ranged from a 2-year-old girl to a 98-year-old woman. As noted earlier, these crimes have become more violent. The case of Anene Booysen was reported in many international sources. She was raped and killed by a former boyfriend and his friends, who broke her fingers, cut her throat, and eviscerated her, leaving her still alive when she was found, though she died soon after (RFI, "Afrique du Sud"). She was one of 65,000 sexual assaults that year in South Africa, with an estimate that only one out of every thirty-six is reported. *Slate Afrique* gives a different estimate of 53,617 rapes per year, or 147 a day, with 49 murders each day, for an annual total of 17,805 murders ("Chiffre affolant"). Maria Malagardis, reporting for the French publication *Liberation*, estimated over a million victims of rape per year in South Africa (Malagardis, "L'Afrique du sud malade"), while the French *Closer Mag* reported the detail that Olympic runner Oscar Pistorius had viewed pornography before he shot his long-term love Reeva Steenkamp (Vincent, "Oscar Pistorius"). After a man raped and strangled a 3-year-old child, there was a large public demonstration in Pretoria against men who rape. About the same time, a 30-year-old confessed to strangling and raping two sisters, ages two and three. Three other men were held for raping and killing an 86-year old Austrian nun in South Africa ("Viol et meurtre"). Carjacking is a common crime in South Africa; other reports mention rapes and murders now accompanying carjackings, as in the case of Hannah, a student who was raped, strangled and stabbed to death by four men (Hyman, "Hannah Cornelius's Last Hours"). President Jacob Zuma declared that the killing of women and children had become a crisis in the country and that South Africa must be made safe for women to live and work (Zuma, "Address by President Jacob Zuma").

On June 20, 2017, several international news sources reported on a case where offenders in South Africa had both filmed a rape they committed and immediately posted it on the web. Three boys, ages fifteen, sixteen, and seventeen, had raped a fourteen-year old girl in Soweto. While this is just one notorious case, it demonstrates a continuation of a pattern seen worldwide, a pattern that includes not only the assault and the choice to film the assault but also the choice to make the material universally available in real time (AFP, "South African Schoolboys in Court").

I am not aware of any source that claims that using pornography drains off sexual desire, so that an increase in pornography would be accompanied by a decrease in sex crimes. At best, those who favor porn might argue for neutrality. Instead, in the midst of this chaos and bloodshed, the pornography industry has attempted to increase its presence in Africa and especially South Africa ("Legalizing Online Porn"; "List of Adult Television Channels"). Seneweb.com reported in 2011 that a new television reality show of pornography allowed viewers to vote on the best amateur porn performed by people who volunteered to be filmed. Supposedly 1,200 people auditioned to participate in this live filming of sex acts, and 120 finalists were chosen by vote ("Une télé-réalité porno"). The winners of the contest were promised an award worth roughly five hundred euros by *Hustler* magazine ("*Hustler*"). Is this story fully credible? Do people volunteer for such a show of their own free will? If they do, the amount of money they were offered shows contempt for the people who participated; it indicates an awareness that there are so many people who are willing to expose themselves and their partners in acts of sexual escalation for a tiny sum. Yes, five hundred euros may be a lot of money in some countries, where earnings of a dollar or euro a day are common. The participants or victims of this scheme are probably being paid, though, for the perpetual use of their images, which can be sold internationally for years to come.

Meanwhile, three major pornography television channels were lobbying to be able to air 24/7 pornography programming in South Africa. The South African court system, as of 2012, had blocked the start of the programming, though the independent government bureau responsible for licensing stations had not yet made a decision. The three networks were Playboy Europe, Adult XXX, and Private Spice ("La Justice Sud Africaine"). The South African National Film Council, joining many other groups, said that, in view of the fact that youths convicted of rape in South Africa "always point to pornography as a source of inspiration," allowing these channels on the air would be adding fuel to a fire already burning (Human Sciences Research Council, "Child Pornography").

This is a case where members of a well-organized and powerful international industry have chosen to enter a market where there is compelling evidence that their product is causing significant harm. Of course, the industry would deny this. It is worth pondering, however, what it means for an industry such as this to exist and to be able to sell its services internationally in the face of the evidence that those services are certainly not harmless or positively healthy. The pornography industry can be compared to the weapons industry, which sells more and more weapons to areas where there is warfare. The weapons industry has as its defense the argument that those who are being attacked need weapons to defend themselves, and that better weapons will defeat older and less-advanced weapons. While that argument has many flaws explored in *Cain's Crime*, at least it seems to have some plausibility. It is hard to imagine making a case that, if rapists often claim that pornography stimulates them to carry out violent sexual assaults on women, then the answer to the problem is to saturate a country with more and more pornography. Again, no one makes the case that having porn available eliminates men's need for live sex with living people.

To put a face to this industry that worked to flood South Africa with additional pornography, at least two of the networks are relatively easy to trace, though revenue data seems to vary. Playboy Enterprises owns a number of subsidiaries. Once, Playboy was a publicly held company, and one could buy stock in the firm. *Playboy Magazine* itself lost much of its circulation over time, perhaps because it stopped printing full nude pictures. However, by the time that decision was made, circulation had already dropped precipitously, perhaps because so much content was available online in full-color video. Hugh Hefner bought back the company in 2011. In 2010, before the buyback, the annual revenue was $215 million, though marketwatch.com stated that the Chinese licensing business alone was worth $1.5 billion in 2014, with a Chinese income stream of about five billion dollars over the past decade (Garcia and Linnane, "Hefner's Playboy Makes Its Money"). Another site pegged Hefner's net worth at fifty dollars at his death ("Playboy Enterprises"). In 1998, Hefner purchased his main rival, Spice Networks, for $55 million. Spice operates twenty-three movie and TV networks internationally (Richmond, "Playboy Snaps Up Rival Spice"). Adult XXX channels, according to one site, belongs to Playboy, though if you click on another site that offers to describe the service, a Russian voice explains the process for installing a connection.

To cut to the chase, the three networks looking to establish themselves in South Africa were all connected to Hugh Hefner in California, the leader of a business with an annual income perhaps in the billions. Hustler, which was started by the American Larry Flynt and promoted the pornography contest in Africa, still publishes as a magazine. There are many other pornographic channels and websites owned by other entrepreneurs. Wikipedia lists ninety-two channels, though its list may not be complete, and any list probably cannot keep up with the development of the industry. Multi-billion-dollar business interests operate pornographic production, publishing, online, film, DVD, and television networks, and make strategic choices about where to invest time, energy, and legal resources to enter new markets. In the face of South Africa being the rape center of the world, with the local courts stating that young rapists and murderers got their ideas from watching porn, American-based pornographic networks lobbied to increase the amount of pornography available in South Africa. The few dollar amounts listed here do not offer a coherent picture of these enterprises. Perhaps Mr. Hefner had partners and business associates who participated in the operation, expansion, and revenues of this global enterprise.

Is it fair to ask the difference between this enterprise and the weapons marketing carried out by Viktor Bout, who violated various international sanctions to sell weapons to terrorists and to a variety of despots? Mr. Bout is just one of a number of notorious weapons dealers who carried out the same kind of business done by major nations, but who did so in contravention of the rules established by those nations. The pornography industry operates in many nations where pornography is illegal. Does it market a product that is lethal in the way that weapons are lethal? Neither a simple yes nor a resounding no are adequate answers to this question, which requires considerable ethical analysis. Mr. Bout was extradited and imprisoned, while Mr. Hefner died in the Playboy Mansion as a very rich man (Garcia and Linnane, "Hefner's Playboy Makes Its Money"; Rao, "Hugh Hefner's Wiki"). Keep in mind that, whether the networks ultimately achieved their ends of providing more televised pornography, South Africa was already awash in porn, and the courts and government had expressed concern about the offenders who testified in court that they drew inspiration and guidance from consuming that pornography.

This story appears to be continuing, although in 2014 a South African court ruled against StarSat's hardcore porn offerings on a pay-for-view channel, and in March 2015, the South African Supreme Court of Appeal ordered the broadcasts to be stopped, with all costs of the litigation to be paid by the network (Ferreira, "No More Nookie").

On October 3, 2017, the Voice of America reported a spike in refugees from the Katanga region of the Democratic Republic of the Congo to Zambia (Schlein, "UN: Huge Surge"). Fewer than four thousand people were involved in the border crossing, which is either a lot or very few, considering the five million people killed in the past decades in what has been described as the World War of Africa, a conflict initiated in 1960 with the destabilizing of the newly independent Republic of the Congo. Apparently, four thousand people moving into Zambia in a short period was considered a notable flight of refugees. The larger war in the Congo has included episodes of genocide in Burundi, Rwanda, the Congo, and Uganda, as well as a nonstop civil war and general series of insurgencies in the Congo. The Congo is considered the runner-up for world rape capital, after South Africa. Perhaps the situation is worse in the Congo, but it is difficult to get accurate counts. This is a case where the instability is so great that one does not find news articles about Playboy and its subsidiaries attempting to set up television networks, although a simple Internet search for "Katanga viol" or "Katanga porno" or some other variant produces a stream of offers from producers who are willing to provide online pornographic films, usually with an emphasis on school-age girls. The unholy trinity of pornography, rape, and murder is clearly present and is not difficult to document, including participation by the large United Nations force that has been attempting to bring a halt to the violence for decades without success.

The situation of girls and women in the Congo, as in many parts of Africa, is exacerbated by long-standing cultural practices that sanction forced marriage, rape, and slavery. Norah Msuya's essay on these practices in the journal *Dignity* lists a number of such practices, most from West Africa and her own Tanzania, but also a number from southern Africa in general. While she reports the existence of many protocols and organizations dedicated to limiting the abuse of women, she also estimates that in 2017 there were 106,000 modern slaves in South Africa, 834,200 in Nigeria (the most populous African nation), and 769,900 in the Democratic Republic of Congo, most of them women and girls. She writes that "it is widely acknowledged that in nearly every African country, women are subjected to second class citizen status" ("Tradition and Culture in Africa," 3). Among these practices are the West African *trokosi*, or slavery to the gods, which can involve a family giving a girl to a temple or local priest in exchange for family forgiveness or healing; *wahaya*, or the practice in Muslim Niger of acquiring a fifth wife to do chores and to serve in other ways; *ukuthwala*, or kidnapping for marriage with the understanding that, once a girl has been raped, her family will not take her back; *kindoki* in the Congo, in which girls and young boys may be enslaved to exorcise evil spirits; and more widely such practices as forced child marriage, female genital mutilation, and an overall preference for sons over daughters who, as in India and China, end up living in some other family or cost money in dowries. Girls Not Brides, an international organization, cites UNICEF figures that estimate that, in the Congo, 10 percent of girls are married by age fifteen, and 37 percent by age eighteen. Girls Not Brides gives a figure of 200,00 raped in the Congo, though it does not specify a period of time for these rapes ("Girls Not Brides"). In 2010, in South Kivu province—the center of much of the recent violence in the Congo—an organization formed to lobby for equality for men and women. The web presence of this group, Women for Equal Chances, or WEC-Congo, appears to be limited.

It should be noted that there are practices in other parts of the world similar to those reported by Msuya. Berhane Ras-Work, in a report written for the UN WomenWatch, describes a series of traditions in Nepal and India according to which girls are given to temples for services "including forced rape" (Ras-Work, "Impact of Harmful Traditional Practices"). These practices go by the names *devadasi*, *deuki*, and *devaki*. Sources differ as to the meaning of some of these terms. *Deusi* and *devaki* may also be names of songs or dances performed by the *devadasi*, or other women dedicated to temples. Ankur Shingal, in an article in the *UCLA Women's Law Journal*, explains that the *devadasi* system of dedicating girls to temples involved girls dedicated at the ages of between eight and sixteen. While the system was "effectively outlawed in 1924," the laws are not enforced, and it was estimated in 2015 that there were between 44,000 and 250,000 *devadasi* in India. These girls are often used as temple prostitutes, with their initiation into sexuality coming as part of their introduction to the temple precincts. While the system is more common in some areas of India than in others, girls are trafficked into the system from other parts of India, and they can become prostitutes who serve wealthy men as well as priests. Because these women are prostituted as part of the religious system, it is probable that their serial rapes are not counted among the nation's crimes of rape. So, whatever numbers are assigned to the problems of femicide, female infanticide, and rape in India, those numbers need to be increased by the number of women who may be "dead" to the world in the sense that they are trapped in a powerful system of official prostitution sanctioned by religious beliefs (Shingal, "Devadasi System").

Moreover, according to a report prepared by UNESCO in 1993, women who are inducted into the *devadasi* system may subsequently be sold to gangs that run brothels. The UNESCO report also identifies a similar system in the Jain faith, whereby there is "forcible ordination of young girls" as Jain nuns, who may find themselves performing the same tasks as Hindu *devadasi*. Presciently, the editor of this report summarizes the point of this book: "The most crucial and terrible aspect of sexual attacks is the fact that the assaults seem to be directed against the female species as a whole." While the UNESCO report does not identify the making of pornography as a feature of *devadasi*, the report does refer to existing bodies of traditional Indian pornography that are part of the temple and literary traditions, and that provide support for the *devadasi* system (Atal and Kosambi, *Violence Against Women*). Both this report and the article in the *UCLA Women's Law Journal* explain that, at some historical period, *devadasi* involved training high-caste women for dancing and singing at specific rituals. Currently, the *devadasi* system appears to focus on the recruitment of Dalit girls, members of the lowest caste, with an emphasis on sexual exploitation. The UNESCO report includes extensive discussions of other continuing cultural practices, including dowry deaths, the burning of brides, and occasional cases of *sati*, in which widows are burned alive on the funeral pyres of their husbands. The International Dalit Solidarity Network publishes its own compilation of data on these topics ("Caste Discrimination"). Taqbir Huda has written on similar issues in Bangladesh (Huda, "On Sexism").

The long civil war in the Congo has produced a variety of kinds of rape, porn, and murder. There is a background of mistreatment, second-class status for women, and a variety of marriage practices that are predatory. Then there is the porn industry, however it may be organized. Next, there are kidnapping and rape as a form of requisitioning. Rebel forces invade villages and demand to have the eligible girls for camp workers and sexual slaves or common-law wives. Rape, porn, and murder are common methods of carrying out war and terrorizing enemy communities. Some of these crimes are part of cultural practices that encourage men to assault women either as individuals or in gang rapes; other crimes are more strategically organized and involve large groups of girls and women victimized together.

Kongo Times reported in 2012, for example, that groups of Congolese village women were attacked by Rwandan troops, who carried out gang rapes in public, cut the women's genitalia with knives, fired guns into their vaginas, and produced films to satisfy markets in Europe, Asia, and the Americas ("RDC: Le Rapport final"; Nolen, "Not Women Anymore"). These incursions by Rwandaphone troops—soldiers speaking Kinyarwanda, the language of Rwanda—have taken place many times, with some in 2009, others in 2015. M. Mulumeoderhwa, in a piece published by the National Library of Medicine, commented more broadly that African male teens are taught to feel entitled to sex from girlfriends, and engage in forced sex, rape, and other forms of sexual exploitations, using porn as a stimulus (Mulumeoderhwa, "Forced Sex"). News reports about continuing rape and sexual exploitation in the Congo are easy to come by. Reports from the US Department of Labor and the Pulitzer Center note that, in the Democratic Republic of Congo, children are recruited for pornography, and local militias demand that villages supply their children (United States Department of Labor, "Findings on the Worst Forms"; Sawyer and Sawyer, "Congo's Children"). *New Internationalist* in 2017 reported that those girls who are not recruited join Mai Mai or armed self-protection groups, which may rape them anyway as part of their membership. The article states that "up to forty percent of the country's school-age child soldiers are girls" who tend to be held in the bush. Of the girls interviewed for the story, 66 percent had been abducted, some by Joseph Kony's Lord's Army. These women are unlikely to be rescued, because they are kept away from areas of direct combat. "Among the 9000 child soldiers freed by the United Nations in the DRC between 2009 and 2015, only seven percent were girls." Those who do return, as mentioned earlier, are often labeled "prostitutes" by their home villages and then ostracized (Olsson, "Congo's Girl Soldiers Struggle").

Trust.org, similarly, reported that 26,000 women had been raped in Kivu Province in 2006, and another 5,000 in 2009. In 2013, 2,700 children were treated medically for problems related to sexual violence. In North Kivu, over a period of four days in the village of Luvuni, 387 women were raped; in 2012, 126 women in girls were raped in Minova, and in some of these cases, the victims were then "raped" with bayonets and gunfire (Batha, "Ravaged by Ebola"). Peter Jones, reporting from Minova, interviewed a soldier who confessed to raping 53 women himself, including five- and six-year-old girls. Most of these women were also raped by others in the group of twenty-five soldiers who had fallen back on the town after losing a battle (Jones, "Congo"). It was in this period that Margot Wallstrom, the UN Special Representative on Sexual Violence in Conflict, called the Congo the "rape capital of the world" (Lloyd-Davies, "Eastern DR Congo"). These reports come from an area so chaotic that data is hard to come by, and figures for rapes or killings probably underrepresent what is actually happening. However, it is clear that no location is safe. In 2009, there was a report that in the central prison in Goma, the primary town in the eastern Congo, twenty women were raped while a group of incarcerated soldiers attempted to break out. What is clear, however, is that pornography is used as a stimulus, rape generally targets women and girls, on some occasions these rapes are filmed with the films marketed, and rape is a weapon of a genocidal war.

Reports published in November 2017 highlight a different kind of rape and pornography in civil war, though it is rape and filming of pornography that is definitely planned in advance. Cecile Allegra, writing in both *Le Monde* and *The Guardian*, reported on rape as a systematic part of the ongoing war in Libya, which sets two regions against one another and also involves battles with and/or against darker-skinned people who live in the deep Libyan desert. This is a war that combines racial, ethnic, religious, historical, and religious elements. Women in captured towns are routinely raped, though it is not clear whether the rapes of women are filmed. What has become a part of the structure of this war is the capture and rape of men by all sides in the conflict. The object of the rapes is to take revenge for prior rapes and to render the male victims impotent in every sense as well as incontinent and so deeply affected by PTSD that they exhibit signs of resignation syndrome or psychogenic catatonia, doing nothing but sleeping and maintaining silence. With great difficulty, interviewers managed to draw accounts from some of these victims, who are so deeply ashamed at being repeatedly sodomized with broomsticks and other instruments that they say they would rather die than testify openly about what was done to them. In one case, a victim reported that, in order to be given food in the prison where he was kept for months, he had to sodomize himself with a broomstick provided for the purpose until he bled. The stick was affixed to the wall and prisoners had to back into it. One man reported being kept in such a prison for four years, sometimes kept naked in the cells, and sometimes forced to rape others on pain of death. These rapes were often filmed on iPhones with the threat that the movies would be posted to the web as a further punishment or as a means of annihilating the spirits and identities of the victims.

These are clearly cases of rape as a form of assassination. These two articles suggest that these practices of capturing, imprisoning, and raping men from the warring groups are widespread, though no numbers of victims were provided. The same articles note that the women of the captured families were also raped—sometimes mothers are raped out in the street and in front of their children, such that the children would no longer speak to their mothers out of great shame. Many of the men and women do not survive, though there are no complete tabulations of this ongoing holocaust (Allegra, "Le Viol"; Allegra, "Subjugate Men").

At some point, of course, it becomes nauseating to add numbers in support of these stories. This book has contained enough numbers. The point is that in Libya, as in Bosnia and the Congo and many other places, rape is used as a weapon, sexual acts are more about violence than pleasure (except for sadistic pleasure and whatever gratification comes from revenge), and pornography is used not only to stimulate the rapes and to provide models for raping, but also to inflict more damage by making the rapes public and even internationally available. What these accounts underline is the fact that pornography is violence. It has always been violence in the sense that it is objectification and dehumanization. It has always been violence in that it leads to violent behavior and teaches young people how to act violently against women. As used in war, pornography is reduced to its essential nature as a tool for inflicting violence and destroying people by hurting and then shaming them into traumatized and nearly paralytic states.

There is a curious passage in Emmanuel Carrere's recent study of early Christianity, *Le Royaume*, or *The Kingdom*. Carrere is a widely published contemporary French novelist and essayist. This book is similar in many ways to other revisionist approaches to the life of Jesus of Nazareth and the theological creativity of Paul the Apostle. One finds related views in studies by Reza Aslan, Albert Schweitzer, and many other scholars and writers on religious history. Carerre always inserts his own biography into his books, and in the case of his book on Christianity, he pauses toward the end to include a discussion of why he likes to look at videos of women masturbating, and how his current lover is aware of and supports his interest in this pornography. The sudden insertion of this pornographic material in an otherwise thoughtful and even passionate discussion of Christianity and true charity is arresting, even shocking. It is difficult to guess Carrere's reasons for this section of his book. Perhaps, as he moves toward his conclusion (that we will find true happiness only in dedicating ourselves to those in need), he wishes to show that he is "one of us," an ordinary person who has sexual fantasies and watches pornography. He's with it; he is not merely a prude, not some kind of saintly figure. Perhaps he wishes to create a sense of greater intimacy with his readers, or to create a contrast between ordinary life and the advocacy of radical charity that he proposes as an end to the spiritual quest. Whatever his reasons, he reflects briefly on all those women who choose to set up cameras, undress, masturbate, and then upload their films to the web, smiling as they do every part of this long process. Perhaps there are ordinary people who, for various reasons, choose to produce their own pornography with themselves or with friends; almost anything seems possible on the Internet, and people certainly learn to victimize themselves. The reason his moment of revelation is worth remarking on at all is that he apparently does not consider that the women on the sites he visits may not have chosen freely to expose themselves. The research on pornographers shows that they demand that their subjects smile. Their business involves violence and human trafficking. In those respects—violence and compulsion—ordinary factory-produced porn is no different from the pornography produced in wars and prisons.

chapter four

AN ENDING

Summarizing the Case

THE OBJECT OF THIS book is to make a case that the world's women live always in the higher stages of Gregory Stanton's eight stages of genocide and that pornography contributes to this constant condition of threatened or active genocide. The cascade of data presented here, drawn from a large number of international organizations, NGOs, government agencies, advocacy groups, and newspapers and magazines must not obscure this simple and basic thesis. Women live under a shadow of genocide.

To make that case, it is first necessary to argue that the huge number of women's deaths constitutes a form of war, because genocide is generally understood to take place during wars, although it is certainly possible for genocide to be carried out systematically against a group, such as an ethnic or religious group, without a state of war or civil war. The recent case of the genocide against the Rohingya Muslim minority of Burma or Myanmar might be considered genocide without a war, though there has in fact been a state of civil war in Myanmar for decades, with various sections and minority groups at war with the central government. I choose, however, to assert that what has been going on globally does in fact constitute a state of war for the following reasons. First, the total number of deaths of women involved for the twentieth century arguably surpasses the number of people killed in that century's major wars, genocides, purges, and mass starvations. A reasonable high estimate for the number of missing women, in cultures that routinely kill female babies and many unwanted brides, is 330,000,000, a number that can be compared to about 250,000,000 victims of wars, purges, and other genocides. The United Nations and several scholars who project numbers of deaths assume with good reason that this killing will proceed at about the same rate for the same cultural reasons, just as there is every reason to believe that this level of killing has been with our species for thousands of years. Second, this war is an organized effort, though there are also many other women killed as a result of spousal murders and in other crimes. Large-scale killing of women is part of long-standing cultural practices. Third, because those cultural practices are well-established and recognized, even where they are formally against laws, it is reasonable to say that the killing is officially sanctioned by virtue of the fact that it is tacitly accepted and, resultingly, it continues. Fourth, women are systematically seriously injured, either physically or psychologically, by acts of violence that do not physically kill them. Rape is an epidemic, culturally organized, prepared for, supported, and tacitly accepted. It is a way to kill the soul or psyche, if not always the body.

Whether one agrees that this war against women meets any particular official or new definition of war, this state of mass killing constitutes genocide. The official definition of genocide adopted by the United Nations refers to women multiple times as a group in order to explain what constitutes genocide. Sadly, that definition neglects to include women as a group among those that can officially be subjected to genocide. This is a logical error on the part of the official definition. It is also a grave moral error, as well as evidence of the eighth stage of genocide: denial that it is happening or has happened. Women as a group are identified and classified as targets, symbolized as less than men, dehumanized in a multitude of ways, and subjected to highly organized discrimination and violence, as well as to violence that is prepared through extensive training of men who kill or rape. Whenever social chaos, war, civil war, or other forms of disorder (including even the relatively small disorder of moving to college) loosen the organization of a society, women are likely to be targeted for violence, both individually and in outbreaks of mass rape and often murder. As a result of all these processes or stages of genocide, women are in fact subjected to an ongoing campaign of genocide that is worse in some places than in others, though it is easy to find advanced stages of genocide against women wherever one looks around the world.

A reasonable objection to the case made here is that the primary numerical evidence is drawn from a relatively small number of cultures where there is a longstanding pattern of female infanticide, leaving smaller total numbers to establish the case with respect to the rest of the world. The populations of the chief nations where there is substantial evidence for femicide, China, India, Pakistan, and Bangladesh, total over three billion of the 7.7 billion people on the Earth, as of 2018. There is limited evidence for continued femicide in some parts of the Arab world, where the prophet Muhammad made a point of condemning the practice. An estimated six million women are killed each year in murders, comparable to the Jewish Holocaust all over again each year. As I argued in *Cain's Crime*, building on the philosophical insight of Joseph Popper-Lynkeus, every human life may have infinite value, so there is no logic by which deaths can be compared. Popper-Lynkeus's once popular ethical theory deserves reconsideration, though this is not the place to explain it beyond stating an abbreviated form of his "motto" or thesis, that any single human life is worth more than the totality of humanity's art and science (Popper-Lynkeus, *Individual and the Value*). Extreme? Not if one gives careful consideration to his case. Consequently, by referencing the Holocaust, I do not mean to compare or to weigh in the same scale the evils of the Holocaust with the everyday and continuing evils of femicide across all cultures.

It is not clear how many women are killed in the dozen or so other nations where there appear to be traditions of femicide, including North Korea, Liberia, Senegal, Nigeria, Nepal, Morocco, Algeria, Tunisia, Syria, Egypt, Jordan, Turkey, and Cameroon. Guatemala has passed a law against femicide, motivated in part by the killings of women during a long civil war and genocide that killed some two hundred thousand Mayan people. Even leaving out the nations where femicide is the highest, there is *abundant* evidence of widespread killing of women. If one adds to these numbers the women who are permanently or significantly damaged by rape and other violence normal within their cultures, the evidence for ongoing genocide against women is even stronger. The Rome Statute of the International Criminal Court, published in 1998, has been interpreted to include rape as a crime of genocide (MacKinnon, personal communication). However, in many respects, the Rome Statute definition is lacking in the same ways as the earlier UN definition. Once again, genocide is defined as "intent to destroy, in whole or part, a national, ethnical, racial or religious group, as such," with no explicit mention of women as a group. Once again, the criteria include "imposing measures intended to prevent births within the group," while not explicitly stating that those measures necessarily include impregnating women with children of a different ethnicity or nationality, or destroying women's ability to bear children, or causing such profound psychological damage to women that they are unlikely ever to conceive. Sexual violence is specifically mentioned only under the part of the Statute that defines crimes against humanity. A recent article by Marie Forestier in the French paper *Liberation*, describes rape as a systematic weapon used against women in areas of Syria that do not support the central government (Forestier, "En Syrie").

A second objection to this argument, of course, is that rape and the violence associated with it, as well as the conception of unwanted children, do not constitute "death" in any meaningful sense. Death has only a single form, when the biological mechanism is permanently arrested. However, even the flawed United Nations definition of genocide allows for the inclusion of widespread rape and the conception of unwanted children as an aspect of genocide, because these are methods that can bring about paralysis, unwanted ethnic mixing (which can destroy the solidarity of a group), long-term post-traumatic stress, and catatonia (what the Swedish authorities have termed "resignation syndrome"). Still, it seems that societies continue to exist in the presence of routine rapes, including, for example, the almost ninety thousand rapes in the United States each year, a figure that may not include all the unreported rapes. As has been argued before, the point of this book is to raise a fundamental question about what kind of a world we have made, where it is possible to manage or to exist in the face of so much violence. How do the 20 percent of female college students in America who are probably victims of rape get on with the business of living in small communities where they share space with those who have raped them, with the business of completing college classes and degrees and preparing for careers, with the business of perhaps marrying and raising children, knowing that a significant number of the men they meet have probably committed date rape or another form of sexual assault? Evidently, women and men throughout the world have managed to continue societies while accommodating femicide and widespread rape that destroys women's lives. William Miller and his colleagues, among others, have written on these issues in "The Effects of Rape on Marital and Sexual Adjustment." L. J. Cohen and Susan Roth offer a picture of the long-term aftereffects of rape ("Psychological Aftermath of Rape"). The reader should also consider why men rape, the role of power in rape, and the problems associated with the treatment of victims (Honan and Replogle, "Why Do Men Rape"; Koss and

Burkhart, "Conceptual Analysis of Rape Victimization"; Murphy, "What Experts Know").

Aside from the fact that the numerical evidence of war and genocide is strong, however one chooses to limit the numbers, the other fact is that the stages of genocide, as defined by Stanton, are obviously present in the lives of the world's women.

Pornography promotes genocide. That is a strong statement, though the evidence argues for its truth. A stronger and equally reasonable claim is that pornography is one of the forms of violence that constitutes the age-long genocide against women. Pornography has been with us since the beginning of the human written record in the *Epic of Gilgamesh*, where the first important woman we meet is the luscious one, a prostitute sent out both to sexually "complete" and to weaken a warrior. Pornography classifies women as sexual objects. Pornography objectifies and dehumanizes women. Pornography is used as a weapon against women, and sometimes against men as well. Pornography is an organized business that perpetuates the dehumanization and objectification of women and supports other cultural traditions that teach those things. Pornography is used to prepare assaults on women, both by individual rapists and murderers and by groups of men, including revolutionaries and college fraternity brothers; pornography is one of the forms that violence takes. Those who argue for the benefits of pornography do so out of the belief that it is a useful method for sexual education and for stimulating satisfying sexual experiences. Because the human written record begins with pornography, it may be hard to imagine what human life would be like without demeaning representations of women. Clearly the record indicates that societies that are more "straightlaced" about pornography include many people who "use" it on the sly. There is no part of the world that does not need to face this issue.

A further point can be made about using the products of the international pornography industry, even if all one does is enjoy one of what the British call "lad's mags." Within the last few years, there has been a movement—particularly on the West Coast of the United States but also in nations such as Uruguay—to legalize the recreational as well as the medical use of marijuana. Marijuana has, of course, been widely used around the world during the years of prohibition, and while some has been grown locally, as in the Upper Peninsula of Michigan or various areas of California like Humboldt County, much of the marijuana used in the United States has been imported from Mexico or other nations by organized cartels that

engage in the weapons trade, money laundering, the sale of more dangerous narcotics, murder, theft, torture, and many other crimes. In the past,
those who used marijuana sometimes conversed about the morality of using that drug when they knew that the suppliers probably engaged in ab-
horrent crimes. I don't know how many people who tried pot ever stopped
smoking it solely because of these moral reservations, or how many good
citizens stopped buying bootlegged alcohol during the American period of
Prohibition because they knew that their liquor was purchased from gangs
that committed a wide range of crimes, including prostitution and human
trafficking. The application of this point to pornography is obvious. The
pornography industry is a multi-billion-dollar international activity that
involves child abuse, kidnapping, enslavement, human trafficking, torture,
battery, and many other crimes. Hugh Hefner's Playboy network of companies included international film companies that received multinational
funding and worked hard to make their products available in places like
South Africa, where there was a clear connection between the consumption
of pornography and an epidemic of rape. Is this not a business that no one
ought to patronize? Anyone who uses pornography gives tacit consent to
all the crimes associated with pornography.

The case is reasonably clear. Women live at all times and in all places
in advanced stages of Stanton's eight stages of genocide. There is a war
against women and genocidal practices in force against women. Pornography contributes significantly to this genocidal war and is one of the forms
of violence used against women.

This book can be restated in terms of a specific theory: Karl Popper's
critical rationalism. The hypothesis is that women are subjected to ongoing
genocide, as defined by the eight stages of genocide from Gregory Stanton.
The data supports the hypothesis because it is clear that those eight stages
are present globally, with strong additional evidence that all of those stages
are part of longstanding social structures, though this book has focused
on current data rather than on making a historical case. Popper believed
in the importance of falsification. The burden is on others to show that
there is no fit between the data and Stanton's taxonomy and to advance
an alternative hypothesis that explains the state of affairs described here.
Correlation is not causation—though high correlation indicates some kind
of causation, and in the case of pornography, the complicating factor is that
pornography is violence itself, stimulates violence, and is then the product
of that violence, used to stimulate and inflict more. What other hypothesis

can explain the phenomena described here and the way of organizing those phenomena by using Stanton's taxonomy?

The Future

In November 2017, the *Guardian* reported on a surprising change to the Miss Peru Contest. Peru has had some of the higher rape statistics in the world. In an article titled "Peru Contestants Cite Violence Figures," the reporter detailed how, at the moment in the contest when candidates normally objectified themselves by reciting their breast, waist, and hip measurements, they stood up and called out recent Peruvian statistics for rape, abuse, and human trafficking: "2,202 cases of femicide reported in the last nine years"; "82 femicides and 156 attempted femicides so far this year"; "more than 25% of girls and teenagers abused in their schools"; "3,114 female victims of trafficking have been registered since 2014." A fully radical change, of course, would mean the end of those meat markets called beauty contests with all of the pressures placed on young women to achieve some kind of ideal, at a cost to other priorities in their lives (Collyns, "Miss Peru Contestants Accuse Country"). Peru has initiated a ban of online pornography (Hopkins, "War against Online Porn").

The future may also include uncovering and addressing still more forms of genocide, particularly what Leonard Shengold called soul murder by childhood abuse. Is this a stretch? On December 14, 2017, the government of Australia released its long-developing study of abuse in that nation to international headlines (Griffith, "Acting on Australia's Landmark Abuse Inquiry"). The report includes *four hundred* recommendations. As reported by the BBC, there are such findings as "up to 60,000 survivors may be eligible for compensation." These are children who were sexually or physically abused by churches—Protestant, Catholic, Jehovah's Witnesses—by schools, day-care centers, sporting clubs, and other organizations. If abuse rolls downhill from one generation to the next, this childhood abuse plants the seeds for some of the more visible violence tallied in this book. These children who are now adults do not turn up in the research of experts like Amartya Sen because they are still physically alive, though profoundly dead. And if one accepts the notion of soul murder, some of these people are dead in a meaningful sense. Is there a connection to pornography in these cases? One would need to read the report in full to examine the question thoroughly. It is telling that three months earlier Peter Vincent, an Australian reporter for the *Telegraph*, wrote about a "harrowing" public speech delivered by an Australian member of parliament who found her husband's collection of child pornography (Vincent, "Australian MP Gives Harrowing Speech").

This is not a psychological study. However, a brief scan of the Internet will reveal hundreds of articles on the psychological consequences of rape and other forms of sexual assault. Koss and Burkhart estimate, apparently for an American audience, a rate of 15 to 22 percent of all women raped, with between 32 and 48 percent of those women seeking psychotherapy at some point to cope with the consequences. Reading the statistics on college rape and other rapes in the United States and in Europe, one must ask what the consequences are for those women should they enter into monogamous relationships and raise male and female children. What are the effects on the overall society when such a large proportion of the people are recovering from victimization of a kind that they may not even wish to admit because of the shame and low self-esteem associated with their suffering? Those American rape statistics, as terrible as they are, do not come near such statistics as 59 percent of men in Papua New Guinea stating that they have committed rape, or the high rates of rape in South Africa, the Congo, and elsewhere in the world, as listed previously.

Heather Murphy and Robbie Couch have written relevant review articles on the characteristics and behavior of men who rape, as has Aditya Gautam. There are many other research articles available on this topic, of course. One trend of interest has been the increase in the number of nations that have changed their legal codes concerning rape. In the past, in many countries, a rapist could escape any punishment for rape by marrying his victim (Couch, "Countries Are Banning Rapists"). Some of the literature on this phenomenon includes reflections by the women themselves who were forced into "shotgun marriages" by their families and then raised large families with the men who violated them. Given the prevalence of spousal abuse in the world, perhaps the coping strategies of these women have analogs in many other marriages. What is to be done, to ask an old and tired question, to address the complex phenomenon of bearing and raising children in a forced marriage with a rapist? What does transparency look like? What does healing look like?

Some nations have attempted to ban various forms of pornography, including Russia and China, if the accounts are accurate, and a recent bill in Peru. The record indicates that Russia banned PornHub, which is the largest provider of online pornography, with viewing in the range of four billion hours per year (Estes, "Russia Just Banned PornHub"). Banning has not appeared to limit access to pornography, however. Estimates of the size of China's porn industry, for example, suggest that any official ban has had little effect on the industry or on the consumption of pornography. The growth of the Internet has made pornography far more widespread. Moreover, the existence of the web has led to a new kind of permanence of images uploaded to the cloud. People who are the victims of revenge porn, whether in personal relationships or as a consequence of victimization by states and rebel groups, know that images placed on the web cannot be expunged. The web is a technological innovation, like nuclear weapons. Once out of Pandora's Box, it cannot be rounded up and sealed away for public safety.

Legal remedies are important, as the pioneering work of Catharine MacKinnon and Celine Bardet prove, though they take a very long time. As this book is being written, another of the cases against a Serbian leader has come to an end with the conviction of Radko Mladic. The verdict comes twenty-three years after the crimes. This is too long if justice is defined partially by its certainty and its swiftness. During this same period, many public figures have been fired or shamed out of their jobs, though their offenses were less than the slaughter of an estimated hundred thousand in Serbia. As of the end of December 2017, the ICTY (the International Criminal Tribunal focusing on crimes in the former Yugoslavia) has technically completed its work, but there can be little doubt that it has only begun. MacKinnon's recent book, *Butterfly Politics*, raises an enormous number of important questions about how law and the idea of precedents in law, legal education, and legal theory need to be reconstituted to take into consideration the actual and unequal status of women in the United States and in the world.

Societal movements such as #MeToo, the recent explosion of statements by women across the world that they also have been sexually assaulted, are an important response, though the task of confronting both pornography and the overall genocidal war on women is daunting. Is there a fear among those who advocate the "healthy" use of pornography that the alternative to free access is a form of prudishness that will imperil sexual expression? It may take a sustained effort of imagination and creativity to conceptualize a world in which women are not represented pornographically and where women have attained status equal to that of men, where they are not automatically oppressed, disregarded, and denied power and worth. Once again, given the fact that the written literary record begins with a pornographic story in which women are either prostitutes or violated virgins, there is an enormous amount of cultural baggage to examine or replace with a different vision of human possibilities. Others have scanned this holocaust; their work can be consulted in the bibliography, including Forder's book *The Longest War*, Cox on the pornography of hatred, Cooper's *Geography of Genocide*, and Heidenrich on methods for intervening and preventing genocide.

The future of this issue is likely to involve hundreds of thousands of small actions. In the city of Everett, north of Seattle along the Salish Sea, a controversy rages that is likely to end in the American Supreme Court. Several coffee stands are staffed by baristas who wear bikinis, or, to cite the city's position, outfits identical to those worn by strippers in adult-only clubs. The coffee stands are owned by a known crime syndicate that operates a "talent" agency and a number of legal strip clubs that have been associated with sex crimes and crimes of violence. The city of Everett has passed legislation banning the baristas' dress, and the baristas have responded with a US Constitution First Amendment defense, claiming that they wear the scanty clothing (required by their employer) as a means of self-expression or speech protected by the Constitution (Carter, "Everett's Bikini Baristas"). The lawyers for the coffee stands have also argued that having the servers dress scantily promotes positive female body images, something our increasingly obese culture can profit by. The city has hired a consultant, Dr. Mary Anne Leyden, from the Sexual Trauma and Psychotherapy Program at the University of Pennsylvania, who has testified to the damage done by objectification of women, the relationship between objectification and violence, and other matters familiar in this book. Dr. Leyden significantly points to a concept familiar in current literary and cultural criticism, the power of the male gaze, which by itself can exercise power and dominance over women who are subjected to evaluation and even a kind of violation by being the objects of regular, sustained, and penetrating stares.

One might insert here a typical defense of literature once considered pornographic, such as the end of James Joyce's *Ulysses*, though Joyce and D. H. Lawrence were tame and cautious compared to more recent literary pornography, with its explicit objectification of women through the description of sexual organs and actions. The question before the courts and society is where the boundaries of freedom should be set. One can be jailed for possessing pornographic pictures of children, yet praised, defended, and highly paid for promoting pornographic images of young adults. The consequences of and violence associated with pornography must be weighed, and a very heavy weight on one side of the scale is the history and reality sketched here, a story of pornography and genocide that reaches into our earliest written record. As of late December 2017, the local courts have so found in favor of the baristas' right to express themselves by wearing the clothing mandated by their employers. In other words, at the moment, this case is going the same direction as the various cases lodged against the pioneering anti-pornography legislation of MacKinnon and Dworkin.

In this author's opinion, the women who serve coffee in those roadside shops outside Seattle are no freer to express their opinions by donning the scanty dress prescribed by their employers than the actresses in pornographic films who are told to smile as they are forced into sexual acts, many of which involve violence.

Catharine MacKinnon's essay on torture in her recent book, *Butterfly Politics*, raises a fundamental question. Child pornography is illegal, partly because children cannot consent. Courts and other authorities around the world have tended to take the view that women have consented to various forms of sexual assault, that they have "asked for it" because they stayed married to an abuser or wore the wrong clothes. The violence committed against women by pornography, as MacKinnon has shown throughout her work, is so severe that it seems reasonable to ask for the following standard: a woman who genuinely wishes to be trafficked in pornography must sign a permission form in circumstances that guarantee that she is acting of her own free will and without any undue pressure or duress. If there is no such form on record, then any pornographic work is illegal. The burden of proof should be placed on the pornographers. This may be an offensive suggestion; the topic itself is barbed with offenses to so many sensibilities. To put the issue this way is merely to ask: what healthy adult woman would, of her own free will, choose to be the subject of the violence that is pornography?

Immanuel Kant's essay *Perpetual Peace* puts this issue in a different way. Government leaders, Kant argues, should always act in private as if all of their actions were performed in full public view. Transparency, Kant thought, would lead to an increase in peace and the morality of government decisions. Kant reasoned that if a leader were ashamed to perform an action or make a particular decision in public view, then that was strong evidence that the action or decision was wrong. It follows that if there is nothing wrong with pornography, then it should be possible to perform

it in public. Neither the performers nor the audience should have any reservations about doing in public what is now made available in specialty
magazines theoretically sold only to adults or in specialized theaters or
websites. Consider that countries around the world permit men and wom-
en to box in public and to fight in other forms of so-called "martial arts"
(with the brief exception of Sweden, which banned the sport for a time).
These performances are governed by rules and commissions, sanctioned
by state and/or national governments, attended by crowds, and filmed and
streamed on the Internet. Societies have decided that raw displays of violence are acceptable, although it is illegal to engage in fist fights in public or
at home. This comes back to the paradox pointed out by Gershon Legman
decades ago. How is it possible that sex between people can be legal in life
but not in the media, while violence in life is illegal, though it is legal and
praised in media presentations? So far as I am aware, however, no government permits live sex shows or live events in which women are subjected to
sexual violence. It is odd, therefore, that films of sexual violence are permissible for both public and private consumption.

Thomas Piketty's study of income inequality discusses whether large
degrees of inequality may lead to political instability. Data and rankings reported earlier in this book point out that women live in a state of significant
economic and political inequality, even in nations like the United States,
where women's access to education and health care is about the same as
men's. Piketty does not specifically address sexual inequality in his book.
It is easy to hypothesize, at least, that increases in women's economic and
political power might lead to decreases in victimization, as it is obvious that
men take advantage of their positions, income, and power to harass women
and to do worse. This is a subject that demands further research. Deidre
McPhillips's presentation in *US News* is an interesting graphic approach to
this and other aspects of the problems women face. Her piece is titled "The
War on Women, in Five Charts."

One way to examine the relationship between income inequality and
violence against women is to look at trends between the latest United Nations data on rape and the latest GINI scores for income inequality. GINI
scores range from zero to 100, where zero would be the score of a nation
where everyone shared equally in everything, and where a score of 100
would mean that one person owned everything. The scores are developed by
a variety of agencies, including the CIA, the United Nations, and the World
Bank ("List of Countries by Income Inequality"). The Wikipedia essay on

this topic offers a data set based on the findings of those three agencies. GINI scores range from a low of about twenty-five in Scandinavian nations to a high of the mid-sixties in South Africa and Namibia. That there is no obvious correlation between violence against women and economic equity can be seen in the fact that Sweden and Iceland, with rounded GINI scores of twenty-seven and twenty-six, are among the nations with the highest levels of rape in the world. In Iceland, there are fifty-four rapes for every one hundred thousand people, and in Sweden the rate is fifty-seven per one hundred thousand, based on data released in 2015. Only seventy or so nations provided data for the UNODC rape study that year, which limits the usefulness of the data. South Africa, with a GINI score of sixty-three, did not report rape data that year, though there is good reason to believe that its epidemic of rape was continuing. Bosnia and Herzegovina had a GINI score of thirty-three, and the Democratic Republic of the Congo had a GINI score of 42.1. Neither nation reported rape data for 2015.

However, looking at the nations that did report rape data, and choosing the eleven nations with the highest rates of rape for which GINI scores are available, perhaps one hypothesis is worth further study. Belgium, Iceland, and Sweden have high rates of rape and low GINI scores. Are they outliers? The other eight nations with top rape rates on record for 2015 have GINI scores from the forties to low fifties. They are places with significant economic inequality: Cape Verde, Jamaica, El Salvador, Panama, Columbia, Guyana, Peru, and the United States of America. In a typical year, the United States has a GINI score close to that of Uganda and South Sudan. The meaning of a GINI score is not the level of poverty or wealth in a nation, but rather how evenly that wealth is distributed. The United States is also interesting in that its GINI score has risen, indicating increasing inequality, since 1968, which was in one sense the year of greatest economic equality in that country, though in other respects it was a year of racial discord and political upheaval over many issues, including the War in Vietnam, the presidential election, and the assassination of several key leaders. To return to the main point, it seems intuitively plausible that if women had more economic and political power, including political power in the workplace, they would live in a less dangerous world.

In this video age, those who explore ideas through television may wish to examine the treatment of this book's themes in their daily viewing. For this purpose, one recent series stands out, perhaps, both because it is somewhat pornographic itself and because it examines in depth the corrosive effects of pornography on society. The series is "Case," a nine-part mystery filmed and developed in Iceland, a nation with one of the highest rates of rape in the world, though one of the lowest rates of murder. The program is pornographic in that it includes footage of naked people, including naked teens. What standards apply to Netflix and other production companies that air their products on the web may be worth investigating. The writers and actors, however, have managed to probe the depths of child abuse, the dangers of pornography, the violence of revenge pornography, and the connections among pornography, alcoholism, drug abuse, and other offenses against human persons. At the opening of this book, I said that I did not watch pornography in the course of research; what appeared in this mystery is an exception to this rule, and one that surprised and troubles me, because the program could have achieved its aims without descending to the level of the problem that it anatomized.

Taking another perspective, consider what has been lost. Denis Guedj was a mathematician and a professor of history and scientific epistemology at the University of Paris. Guedj's charming romp through the history of mathematics, *Le theoreme du perroquet*, or *The Parrot's Theorem*, is a mystery novel that covers the stories of the major contributors to the development of mathematics from Thales in ancient Greece to the late twentieth century. Of the 155 mathematicians listed at the end of the volume, only two were women. One published under a male name. The other was Hypatia of Alexandria, who was tortured by having her skin scraped away with the sharp edges of sea shells, after which she was burned by a mob. The absence or limited number of women in other professions, arts, and sciences is similar. This is the right moment to remember, as well, Olympe de Gouges, the pioneering French feminist who insisted that women be granted the same rights as men in the French Revolution and was beheaded in the Reign of Terror in 1793.

What would the world look like if this war were to end? The question is far beyond the scope of this book. Herbert Marcuse ended his *Essay on Liberation* with the following thought: "what are the people in a free society going to do? The answer which, I believe, strikes at the heart of the matter was given by a young black girl. She said: for the first time in our life, we shall be free to think about what we are going to do" (91). (While I may be mistaken in this attribution, I believe the black woman was Marcuse's student Angela Davis.) The statement might be modified to read as follows: what are the people in an egalitarian society going to do, a society where women and men are truly equal? Catharine MacKinnon's *Toward a Feminist Theory of the State* ponders some of the possibilities. The point of this book has merely been to make the case that the war is real, that it is genocidal, and that it is enflamed by pornography.

We practice genocide against half our species, and we whet our appetites for violence and sexual assault with pornography. At an absolute minimum, the legal boundaries for what constitutes acceptable sexuality in the media need to be moved. No doubt, in addition to whatever other faults this book contains, it has only scratched the surface of the issues and the evidence. What a world you bequeathed to us, Gilgamesh. How little we have made of it.

BIBLIOGRAPHY

"2002 Gujarat Riots." https://en.wikipedia.org/wiki/2002_Gujarat_riots.

"2008 Kandhamal Nun Gang-Rape Case: 3 People Convicted, 6 Acquitted." *Times of India*, March 14, 2014. https://timesofindia.indiatimes.com/india/2008-Kandhamal-nun-gang-rape-case-3-people-convicted-6-acquitted/articleshow/31998696.cms.

Abdelaziz, Salma. "'It Would Be Good if I Too Died:' Rape as a Weapon of War against the Rohingya." https://www.cnn.com/2017/11/17/asia/myanmar-rohingya-rape.

Adan, Fartuun Abdisalaan. "Somalia's Shocking Response to a Rape Report." *Huffington Post*, February 22, 2013. https://www.huffingtonpost.com/fartuun-abdisalaan-adan/somalias-rape-report_b_2742382.html.

"Afghan Soldiers Are Using Boys as Sex Slaves, and the U.S. Is Looking the Other Way." https://www.washingtonpost.com/news/global-opinions/wp/2017/07/18/afghan-soldiers-are-using-boys-as-sex-slaves-and-the-u-s-is-looking-the-other-way/?utm_term=.d11723a92c36?

"Afghanistan: Events of 2016." https://www.hrw.org/world-report/2017/country-chapters/afghanistan#d91ede.

AFP. "Afrique du Sud: prison à perpétuité pour un viol et un meurtre" ["South Africa: Life Imprisonment for Rape and Murder"]. *Jeune Afrique*, November 1, 2013. https://www.jeuneafrique.com/depeches/28014/politique/afrique-du-sud-prison-a-perpetuite-pour-un-viol-et-un-meurtre/.

———. "L'Afrique du Sud malade de ses viols" ["South Africa Sick of Rapes"]. *Le Point*, February 26, 2013. https://www.lepoint.fr/societe/l-afrique-du-sud-malade-de-ses-viols-26-02-2013-1632568_23.php.

———. "South African Schoolboys in Court after Filming Teen Rape." *Daily Nation*, June 20, 2017. https://www.nation.co.ke/news/africa/South-African-schoolboys-court-filming-teen-rape/1066-3978244-j49lxfz/index.html.

"Aftermath of Shahadat." http://babrimasjid.tripod.com/aftermath.htm.

Alexander, Michelle. *The New Jim Crow: Mass Incarceration in the Age of Colorblindness*. New York: New Press, 2014.

Allegra, Cecile. "Le Viol, Arme de Guerre en Libye" ["Rape, Weapon of War in Libya"]. *Le Monde*, November 3, 2017.

———. "Subjugate Men: Libyan Militants Use Male Rape as a Weapon of War." *Guardian*, November 4, 2017.

Allen, John L., Jr. "'Kandhamal' Tells the Whole Story of Anti-Christian Persecution." *Crux*, July 28, 2015. https://cruxnow.com/faith/2015/07/28/kandhamal-tells-the-whole-story-of-anti-christian-persecution.

Ambrosino, Brendan. "The Invention of Heterosexuality." *BBC Future*, March 16, 2017. http://www.bbc.com/future/story/20170315-the-invention-of-heterosexuality.

American Psychological Association. "By the Numbers: Men and Depression." https://www.apa.org/monitor/2015/12/numbers.aspx.

Amran, Athman. "50 Underage Girls 'Sold Weekly' as Sex Workers in Kenya." *Standard Digital*, October 5, 2011. https://www.standardmedia.co.ke/article/2000044145/50-underage-girls-sold-weekly-as-sex-workers-in-kenya.

Anderson, Liz. "Fraternities' Link to Rape Should Not be Ignored." *Daily Texan*, April 18, 2017. http://www.dailytexanonline.com/2017/04/18/fraternities%E2%80%99-link-to-rape-should-not-be-ignored.

"Annual Reports to Human Rights Council and General Assembly." www.ohchr.org/en/issues/children/pages/annualreports.aspx.

"APA Review Confirms Link between Playing Violent Video Games and Aggression." *APA News*, August 13, 2015. https://www.apa.org/news/press/releases/2015/08/violent-video-games.aspx.

Aslan, Reza. *The Zealot*. New York: Random, 2013.

Atal, Yogesh, and Meera Kosambi, ed. *Violence Against Women: Reports from India and the Republic of Korea*. RUSHAP Series of Monographs and the Occasional Papers 37. Bangkok: UNESCO Principal Regional Office for Asia and the Pacific, 1993. https://unesdoc.unesco.org/ark:/48223/pf0000096629?posInSet=1&queryId=69ff8 2ca-056c-43ae-b845-5a71cb17dd13.

"Australia Child Abuse Inquiry: Final Recommendations Released." *BBC News*, December 15, 2017. www.bbc.com/news/world-australia-42361874.

Baer, Drake. "There Are 3 Kinds of Porn Users." *Cut*, March 7, 2017. https://www.thecut.com/2017/03/the-difference-between-healthy-and-unhealthy-porn-use.html.

"Bacha Bazi." https://en.wikipedia.org/wiki/Bacha_bazi.

Bailey, Bob. Personal communication, August 2018.

Banerjee, Sikata. *Make Me a Man! Masculinity, Hinduism, and Nationalism in India*. New York: State University of New York Press, 2005.

Bardet, Celine. "Celine Bardet.com." www.celine-bardet.com.

———. *Zones Sensibles: Une femme en lutte contre les criminels de guerre* [*Sensitive Areas: A Woman against War Criminals*]. Paris: Editions du Toucan, 2011.

Batha, Emma. "Ravaged by Ebola and War, Congo Named Most Neglected Crisis of 2018." *Thomas Reuters Foundation News*, December 20, 2018. http://news.trust.org//item/20181219235550-shh2x.

Benard, Cheryl. "I've Worked with Refugees for Decades. Europe's Afghan Crime Wave Is Mind-Boggling." *National Interest*, July 11, 2017. https://nationalinterest.org/feature/ive-worked-refugees-decades-europes-afghan-crime-wave-mind-21506.

Berlinger, Joshua, et al. "U.N. Peacekeepers Accused of Raping Civilians." *CNN*, April 6, 2016. www.cnn.com/2016/04/06/africa/united-nations.

Bern, Claude, dir. *Germinal*. Renn Productions, 1993.

Bern, Sandra. "Gender Polarization." In *The Lenses of Gender: Transforming the Debate on Sexual Inequality*, 80–132. New Haven: Yale University Press, 1993.

Bernama, the Malaysian News Agency. Cambodia's HIV Infection Rate Highest in Asia. December 1, 1998.

Berrios, Rocio Portela. "Communities Torn Apart by Genocide and the Sex Trafficking Industry." https://www.internationaljusticeproject.com/communities-torn-apart-by-genocide-and-the-sex-trafficking-industry/.

Bongaarts, John, and Christophe Z. Guilmoto. "How Many More Missing Women? Excess Female Mortality and Prenatal Sex Selection, 1970–2050." https://onlinelibrary.wiley.com/doi/full/10.1111/j.1728-4457.2015.00046.x.

Bornman, Elirea. *Violence in South Africa: A Variety of Perspectives*. Pretoria: Human Resources Research Council, 1998.

Bouchaud, Melodie. "Congo Accuses Rwandan Army of Crossing Border and Injuring Soldier." *Vice News*, April 23, 2015. https://news.vice.com/en_us/article/qvag9x/congo-accuses-rwandan-army-of-crossing-border-and-injuring-solider.

Brennan, William. "Female Objects of Semantic Dehumanization and Violence." http://www.fnsa.org/v1n3/brennan1.html.

Brown, Jessica. "Is Porn Harmful? The Evidence, the Myths and the Unknowns." *BBC Future*, September 26, 2017. http://www.bbc.com/future/story/20170926-is-porn-harmful-the-evidence-the-myths-and-the-unknowns.

Buber, Martin. *I and Thou*. New York: Scribners, 1970.

Bureau of Justice Statistics. "Rape and Sexual Assault." https://www.bjs.gov/index.cfm?ty=tp&tid=317.

Burnett, John. "More Stories Emerge of Rapes in Post-Katrina Chaos." *NPR*, December 21, 2005. https://www.npr.org/templates/story/story.php?storyId=5063796.

Busari, Stephanie. "Charity: Aid Workers Raping, Abusing Children." *CNN*, May 27, 2008. http://www.cnn.com/2008/WORLD/europe/05/27/charity.aidworkers/index.html.

Caldwell, Dan, and Robert E. Williams Jr. *Seeking Security in an Insecure World*. New York: Rowman & Littlefield, 2012.

Callan, Aela. "It's a Man's World: Rape in Cambodia." *Al Jazeera*, December 12, 2016. https://www.aljazeera.com/programmes/rewind/2016/12/man-world-rape-cambodia-161212122925546.html.

Callimachi, Rukmini. "Freed from ISIS, Yazidi Women Return in 'Severe Shock.'" *New York Times*, July 27, 2017. https://www.nytimes.com/2017/07/27/world/middleeast/isis-yazidi-women-rape-iraq-mosul-slavery.html.

"Cambodia's HIV Rate Ranks Highest in Asia." *AIDS Alert* 14.11 (Nov 1999) 1–2. https://www.ncbi.nlm.nih.gov/pubmed/11366984.

"Campus Sexual Assault." https://en.wikipedia.org.wiki/campus-sexual-assault.

Carr, Joetta, and Karen M. VanDeusen. "Risk Factors for Male Sexual Aggression on College Campuses." *Journal of Family Violence* 19.5 (October 2004) 279–89.

Carrere, Emmanuel. *La Royaume* [*The Kingdom*]. Paris: Folio, 2014.

Carroll, Jason S., et al. "Generation XXX: Pornography Acceptance and Use Among Emerging Adults." *Journal of Adolescent Research* 23.1 (January 2008) 6–30.

Carter, Mike. "Everett's Bikini Baristas Head to Federal Court to Argue for Freedom of Exposure." *Seattle Times*, November 20, 2017. https://www.seattletimes.com/seattle-news/crime/everetts-bikini-baristas-head-to-federal-court-to-argue-for-freedom-of-exposure/.

"Caste Discrimination and Human Rights." Copenhagen: The International Dalit Solidarity Network, 2015. Idsn.org/wp-content/uploads/2015/12/UNcompilation2.pdf.

Castleman, Michael. "How Much of Porn Depicts Violence Against Women?" *Psychology Today*, June 15, 2016. https://www.psychologytoday.com/us/blog/all-about-sex/201606/how-much-porn-depicts-violence-against-women.

Center for Reproductive Rights. "Women's Reproductive Rights in Cameroon: A Shadow Report." https://www.reproductiverights.org/sites/crr.civicactions.net/files/documents/Cameroon%20CESCR%201999.pdf.

Chaturvedi, Swati. "Modi Must End His Support of Islamophobic, Sexist Trolls." *Huffington Post*, January 10, 2017. https://www.huffingtonpost.com/entry/modi-trolls_us_586bd5b8e4bode3a08f99630.

"Chiffre affolant, il se produit 49 meurtres par jour en Afrique du Sud" ["A Staggering 49 Murders Occur Every Day in South Africa"]. *Slate Afrique*, October 1, 2015. http://www.slateafrique.com/619163/afrique-du-sud-49-meurtres-par-jour.

"Child Sex Trafficking—As Easy in Seattle As Ordering a Pizza." *MyNorthwest*, April 13, 2017. http://mynorthwest.com/5349/child-sex-trafficking-as-easy-in-seattle-as-ordering-a-pizza/?

"Chinese Restaurants Offer Bra Size Discounts." *BBC News*, August 7, 2017. https://www.bbc.com/news/blogs-news-from-elsewhere-40851224.

"CIA Factbook—Sudan." https://www.cia.gov/library/publications/the-world-factbook/geos/su.html.

City News Service. "Genocide in Guatemala Topic of USC International Conference." *Daily Bulletin*, September 11, 2016. https://www.dailybulletin.com/2016/09/11/genocide-in-guatemala-topic-of-usc-international-conference/.

Cohen, Lawrence J., and Susan Roth. "The Psychological Aftermath of Rape: Long Term Effects and Individual Differences in Recovery." *Journal of Social and Clinical Psychology* 5.4 (1987) 523–34.

Colavito, Jason. "The Epic of Gilgamesh." http://www.jasoncolavito.com/epic-of-gilgamesh.html.

Collyns, Dan. "Miss Peru Contestants Accuse Country of Not Measuring Up on Gender Violence." *Guardian*, November 2, 2017. https://www.theguardian.com/global-development/2017/nov/01/miss-peru-2017-contestants-accuse-country-of-failing-to-measure-up-gender-violence.

Committee on the Elimination of Discrimination Against Women. "Concluding Observations on the Combined Fourth and Fifth Periodic Reports of Cameroon." https://tbinternet.ohchr.org/_layouts/treatybodyexternal/download.aspx?symbolno=CEDAW/C/CMR/CO4-5&Lang=en.

Cooper, Allan D. *The Geography of Genocide*. Lanham: University Press of America, 2009.

Corner, Natalie. "The Young British Pakistani Women Prepared to Marry Their COUSINS in Order to Keep Their Families Happy—but Risk Giving Birth to Disabled Children." *Daily Mail*, July 7, 2017. https://www.dailymail.co.uk/femail/article-4674136/The-British-Pakistani-women-marrying-COUSINS.html.

"Cosmetics Industry - Statistics & Facts." https://www.statista.com/topics/3137/cosmetics-industry/.

Couch, Robbie. "Countries Are Banning Rapists from Marrying Their Victims to Avoid Punishment: Report." *Huffington Post*, February 23, 2015. https://www.huffingtonpost.com/2015/02/23/rape-equality-now-report_n_6722928.html.

Covert, Bryce. "Trump Bragged That He Walked in on Naked Beauty Pageant Contestants." *Think Progress*, October 12, 2016. https://thinkprogress.org/trump-beauty-pageants-naked-2dc4b6c6d507/.

Cox, William John. "The Pornography of Hatred." *CounterPunch*, October 8, 2015. https://www.counterpunch.org/2015/10/08/the-pornography-of-hatred/.

"Crime Index for Country 2016 Mid-Year." https://www.numbeo.com/crime/rankings_by_country.jsp?title=2016-mid.

"Crime Index for Country 2017." https://www.numbeo.com/crime/rankings_by_country.jsp?title=2017.

Daily Mail. "US Soldiers and Contractors Sexually Abused 54 Under Age Colombian Girls and Even Made Their Assaults into Pornography and Will Never Face Charges, Report Claims." *Daily Mail*, March 25, 2015. https://www.dailymail.co.uk/news/article-3010496/US-troops-contractors-sexually-abused-54-age-Colombian-girls-assaults-pornography-never-face-charges-report-claims.html.

Darby, Samantha. "Tim Kaine's Response to the Election: Results Give Hope, Despite the Devastating Loss." *Romper*, November 9, 2016. https://www.romper.com/p/tim-kaines-response-to-the-election-results-give-hope-despite-the-devastating-loss-22081.

Dardeen, Lizzie. "'Rampant' Violence against Women in Pakistan Revealed as Groups Fight 'Un-Islamic' Law against Domestic Abuse." https://www.independent.co.uk/news/world/asia/rampant-violence-against-women-in-pakistan-revealed-as-groups-fight-un-islamic-law-against-domestic-a6969311.html.

"Dark Figure of Crime." https://en.wikipedia.org/wiki/Dark_figure_of_crime.

"Dark Side of Peacekeeping." *Independent*, July 10, 2003. https://www.independent.co.uk/news/world/politics/dark-side-of-peacekeeping-95444.html.

Dawes, Andrew and Advaita Govender. "The Use of Children in Pornography in South Africa." Paper presented at the Human Sciences Research Conference, Birchwood Conference Centre, Benoni, South Africa, September 27–28, 2007. http://ecommons.hsrc.ac.za/bitstream/handle/20.500.11910/5791/4883_Dawes_Childpornography.pdf?sequence=1&isAllowed=y.

Dawson, Hannah. "Cambridge Footballers Punished by Jesus College for Chanting about Rape and Sexual Assault." *Cambridge Tab*, June 20, 2016. https://thetab.com/uk/cambridge/2017/06/20/jesus-responds-football-misogyny-scandal-96309.

Dayras, Michèle. "China—Tibet: Genocide Becomes Gynocide." www.genreenaction.net/chine-tibet-quand-le-genocide-devient-un-gynecide.html.

Defoe, Daniel. *Roxana*. Edited by John Mullan. Oxford World Classics Series. London: Oxford University Press, 1996.

Delbyck, Cole. "Jennifer Lawrence Recalls Standing in 'Degrading' Nude Lineup for Audition." *Huffington Post*, October 17, 2017. https://www.huffingtonpost.in/2017/10/17/jennifer-lawrence-recalls-standing-in-degrading-nude-lineup-for-audition_a_23246893/.

Denhollander, Rachel. "U.N. Exposes North Korea's Rampant Forced Abortions, Sterilizations, Infanticide, and Persecution of the Disabled." *LiveAction*, February 18, 2014. https://www.liveaction.org/news/less-than-human-north-koreas-rampant-forced-abortions-sterilizations-infanticide-and-persecution-of-the-disabled/

Department of Veterans Affairs. "PTSD: National Center for PTSD." https://www.ptsd.va.gov.

Dines, Gail. *Pornland: How Porn Has Hijacked our Sexuality*. Boston: Beacon, 2011.

"Discrimination against the Girl Child." http://yapi.org/childrens-rights/discrimination-against-the-girl-child/.

"Domestic Violence in Pakistan." https://en.wikipedia.org/wiki/Domestic_violence_in_Pakistan.

Doughty, Eleanor. "Lad Culture at University Strikes Again." *Telegraph*, October 10, 2014. https://www.telegraph.co.uk/education/universityeducation/student-life/11153365/Lad-culture-at-university-strikes-again.html.

Downes, Alexander B. *Targeting Civilians in War*. Ithaca: Cornell University Press, 2008.

"DR Congo: Mass Rape in Goma Prison." *ReliefWeb*, June 24, 2009. https://reliefweb.int/report/democratic-republic-congo/dr-congo-mass-rape-goma-prison.

Dworkin, Andrea. *Life and Death: Unapologetic Writings on the Continuing War against Women*. London: Free, 1997.

Eleftheriou-Smith, Loulla-Mae. "Gang Rape Video of 16-Year-Old Somali Girl Sparks Outrage and Leads to £7,000 in Donations." *Independent*, January 18, 2017. https://www.independent.co.uk/news/world/africa/gang-rape-somalia-16-year-old-girl-victim-video-attack-outrage-7000-donations-a7532891.html.

The Epic of Gilgamesh. https://archive.org/details/TheEpicofGilgamesh_201606.

"*Epic of Gilgamesh*." https://en.wikipedia.org/wiki/Epic_of_Gilgamesh.

Epstein, Deborah. "La majorite des tueries de mass sont le fait d'hommes auteurs de violences domestiques" ["The Majority of Gunmen Are Also Perpetrators of Domestic Violence"]. *Le Monde*, November 14, 2017. www.lemonde.fr/idees/article/2017/11/14/la-majorite-des-tueries-de-masse-sont-le-fait-d-hommes-auteurs-de-violence-domestiques_5214757_3232.html.

ERA. "Equal Rights Amendment." www.equalrightsamendment.org.

Estes, Adam Clark. "Russia Just Banned PornHub." *Gizmodo*, September 8, 2015. https://gizmodo.com/russia-just-banned-pornhub-1729319986.

"Ethnicity Facts and Figures." https://www.ethnicity-facts-figures.service.gov.uk/.

Eveleth, Rose. "Liechtenstein Has the Most Skewed Ratio of Baby Boys and Girls in the World Right Now." *Smart News*, September 17, 2013. https://www.smithsonianmag.com/smart-news/liechtenstein-has-the-most-skewed-ratio-of-baby-boys-and-girls-in-the-world-right-now-8176140/.

"Eyewitness News." Ewn.co.za/topic/child-pornography-cases.

Fanon, Frantz. *The Wretched of the Earth*. New York: Grove, 1964.

Fantz, Ashley. "Outrage Over 6-Month Sentence for Brock Turner in Stanford Rape Case." *CNN*, June 7, 2016. https://www.cnn.com/2016/06/06/us/sexual-assault-brock-turner-stanford/index.html.

"Federal Shariat Court." https://en.wikipedia.org/wiki/Federal_Shariat_Court.

Feldman, Jamie. "There Were a Lot of Vulvas Showing at Namilia's New York Fashion Show." *Huffington Post*, September 11, 2017. https://www.huffpost.com/entry/vagina-fashion-show_n_59b68c85e4b0b5e531079206.

"Female Infanticide in Pakistan." https://en.wikipedia.org/wiki/Female_infanticide_in_Pakistan.

"Female Infanticide—Study—Country Data." https://wunrn.com/2016/07/female-infanticide-study-country-data/.

Ferguson, James. *The World's Most Dangerous Place: Inside the Outlaw State of Somalia*. Philadelphia: Da Capo, 2013.

Ferran, Lee, et al. "Jihadists' Computers '80 Percent' Full of Porn, Ex-Official Says." *ABC News*, July 14, 2016. https://abcnews.go.com/International/jihadists-computers-80-percent-full-porn-official/story?id=40564987.

Ferreira, Thinus. "No More Nookie on SA Pay-TV Service." *Channel 24*, March 25, 2015. https://www.channel24.co.za/tv/news/no-more-nookie-on-SA-pay-tv-service-20150326.

"Fight the New Drug." www.fightthenewdrug.org.

Film & Publication Board. http://www.fpb.org.za/.

Forestier, Marie. "En Syrie, 'baiser toutes les femmes pour les punir'" ["In Syria, Rape all the Women to Punish Them"]. *Liberation*, March 18, 2018. https://www.liberation. fr/planete/2018/03/18/en-syrie-baiser-toutes-les-femmes-pour-les-punir_1637123.

Fossett, Katelyn. "How Does a Country Develop a 60 Percent Rape Rate?" *Foreign Policy*, September 11, 2013. https://foreignpolicy.com/2013/09/11/how-does-a-country-develop-a-60-percent-rape-rate/.

Foundation for Individual Rights in Education. "Yale University: Fraternity Suspended Five Years for 'Intimidated' Satirical Chant." https://www.thefire.org/cases/yale-university-fraternity-suspended-five-years-for-intimidating-satirical-chant/.

France, Lisa Respers. "Reese Witherspoon, America Ferrera Open Up about Sexual Assault." *CNN Entertainment*, October 18, 2017. https://www.cnn.com/2017/10/17/ entertainment/reese-witherspoon-america-ferrera-assaults/index.html.

Garcia, Tonya, and Ciara Linnane. "Here's How Hugh Hefner's Playboy Makes Its Money." *Market Watch*, October 14, 2015. https://www.marketwatch.com/story/heres-how-hugh-hefners-playboy-makes-it-money-2015-10-13.

Gardam, Judith. *Necessity, Proportionality and the Use of Force by States*. Cambridge Studies in International and Comparative Law 35. Cambridge: Cambridge University Press, 2004.

———. *Non-Combatant Immunity as a Norm of International Humanitarian Law*. Dordrecht: Nijhoff, 1993.

Gastrow, Peter. "Termites at Work: Transnational Organized Crime and State Erosion in Kenya." https://www.ipinst.org/images/pdfs/ipi_epub-kenya-toc.pdf.

Gautam, Aditya. "Why Do Men Rape?" *India Times*, December 16, 2016. https://www. indiatimes.com/lifestyle/why-do-men-rape-259664.html.

Gebreiyosus, Yonas. *Women in African Refugee Camps: Gender Based Violence against Female Refugees: The Case of Mai Ayni Refugee Camp, Northern Ethiopia*. Hamburg: Anchor Academic Publishing, 2014.

"The Gender Ads Project." www.genderads.com/styled-10/photos-34.

"Gender Polarization." https://en.wikipedia.org/wiki/Gender_polarization.

Geneva Declaration on Armed Violence and Development. "Global Burden of Armed Violence 2015: Every Body Counts." http://www.genevadeclaration. org/measurability/global-burden-of-armed-violence/global-burden-of-armed-violence-2015.html.

Gerig, Bruce L. "David & Jonathan and the Epic of Gilgamesh, Part 1: Homosexuality and the Bible." http://epistle.us/hbarticles/gilepic1.html.

Gettleman, Jeffrey. "Sudan Court Fines Woman for Wearing Trousers." *New York Times*, September 9, 2009. www.nytimes.com/2009/09/08/world/africa/08sudan.html.

Gilbert, William S., and Arthur S. Sullivan. *H.M.S. Pinafore*. New York: Alfred Music, 1999.

Gilmore, Jane. "Latest Porn Statistics Are Surprising." *Sydney Morning Herald*, April 24, 2018. https://www.smh.com.au/lifestyle/life-and-relationships/latest-porn-statistics-are-surprising-20180424-p4zbd8.html.

"Girls Not Brides." https://www.girlsnotbrides.org/child-marriage/democratic-republic-of-the-congo.

Gladkov, Fyodor Vasilievich. *Cement*. Chicago: Northwestern University Press, 1994.

Gloege, Danika. "The Shackles That Enslave Child Soldiers." https://wordpress.clarku.edu/id252-ss/2015/11/12/the-shackles-of-slavery-that-bind-child-soldiers/.

Goldsmith, Belinda. "Factbox: Which Are the World's 10 Most Dangerous Countries for Women?" https://www.reuters.com/article/us-women-dangerous-poll-factbox/factbox-which-are-the-worlds-10-most-dangerous-countries-for-women-idUSKBN1JMo1Z.

Goldstein, Joseph. "U.S. Soldiers Told to Ignore Sexual Abuse of Boys by Afghan Allies." *New York Times*, September 20, 2015. https://www.nytimes.com/2015/09/21/asia/us-soldiers-told-to-ignore-sexual-abuse-of-boys-by-afghan-allies.

Gray, John. "John Gray: Steven Pinker Is Wrong about Violence and War." *Guardian*, March 13, 2015. https://www.theguardian.com/books/2015/mar/13/john-gray-steven-pinker-wrong-violence-war-declining.

Gray, Josephus Moses. "Liberia: Gender Inequality—A Major Threat to Women's Progress in Male Dominates Political Society of Liberia." Front Page Africa, April 2, 2017. https://allafrica.com/stories/201704030841.html.

Green, Sarah Jean. "Strangulation is a Powerful Tool of Violence That Often Leaves No Physical Mark; Officials in King County Want It Noticed, Prosecuted." *Seattle Times*, November 13, 2017. https://www.seattletimes.com/seattle-news/crime/king-county-fights-to-stop-strangulations/.

Griffith, Hywel. "Acting on Australia's Landmark Abuse Inquiry." *BBC News*, December 15, 2017. https://www.bbc.com/news/world-australia-42334381.

Guatemala. www.state.gov/j/dvl/r/s/hrrpt/wha/265590.html.

Guedj, Denis. *Le theoreme du perroquet* [*The Parrot's Theorem*]. Paris: Points, 1998.

Gupta, Smita. "Durga Vahini, the 'Moral Police.'" *Hindu*, February 5, 2013. https://www.thehindu.com/news/national/durga-vahini-the-moral-police/article4379616.ece.

Hasinoff, Amy Adele. "The Policy That the US Porn Industry Has and Facebook Needs." *CNN*, November 18, 2017. https://www.cnn.com/2017/11/18/opinions/facebook-policy-revenge-porn-hasinoff-opinion/index.html.

Heidenrich, John G. *How to Prevent Genocide: A Guide for Policymakers, Scholars, and the Concerned Citizen*. Westport: Praeger, 2001.

"Higher Education and Women: Issues and Perspectives." www.unesco.org/education/educprog/wche/principal/women.html.

"Homocide Statistics by Gender." https://en.wikipedia.org/wiki/Homicide_statistics_by_gender.

Honan, Sarah, and Elaine Replogle. "Why Do Men Rape?" *Women News Network*, June 2, 2015. https://womennewsnetwork.net/2015/06/02/why-do-men-rape/.

"Honour Based Violence Awareness Network." http://hbv-awareness.com/.

Hopkins, Curt. "The War against Online Porn Spreads to Peru." *Daily Dot*, August 1, 2013. https://www.dailydot.com/news/peru-online-porn-ban/.

Huda, Taqbir. "On Sexism, Son Preference and Female Infanticide in Bangladesh." *Daily Star*, August 19, 2017. https://www.thedailystar.net/opinion/society/sexism-son-preference-and-female-infanticide-bangladesh-1450642.

"Hudood Ordinances." https://en.wikipedia.org/wiki/Hudood_Ordinances.

Hughes, Donna M. "'Welcome to Rape Camp': Sexual Exploitation and the Internet in Cambodia." *Journal of Sexual Aggression* 6.1–2 (2000) 29–51.

Human Sciences Research Council. "Child Pornography in the Age of the Internet." http://www.hsrc.ac.za/en/review/November-2007/child-pornography.

"*Hustler*." https://en.wikipedia.org/wiki/Hustler.

Hyman, Aron. "Hannah Cornelius's Last Hours . . . by One of the Men Accused of Killing Her." *Times Live*, October 10, 2018. www.timeslive.co.za/news/south-africal/2018-10-10-hannah-corneliuss-last-hours-by-one-of-the-men-accused-of-killing-her/.

India United Against Fascism. "India: The BJP, Rape and the Status of Women." *openDemocracy 50.50*, November 26, 2013. https://www.opendemocracy.net/5050/india-united-against-fascism/india-bjp-rape-and-status-of-women.

"Indian Politicians' 'Unfortunate' Rape Remarks." *BBC News*, June 12, 2014. https://www.bbc.com/news/world-asia-india-27808722.

"Inside an Indian Camp for Radical Hindu Women." *BBC News*, November 9, 2014. https://www.bbc.com/news/world-asia-india-29798148.

"International Association of Genocide Scholars." https://www.genocidescholars.org/.

"International Justice Mission, 2013 Annual Report." https://www.ijm.org/sites/default/files/download/IJM-2013-Annual-Report_Downloadable.pdf.

"Irish Center for Human Rights." http://www.burmalibrary.org/docs09/ichr_rohingya_report_2010.pdf.

The Irrawaddy. "Murky Waters: Burma's Law on Pornography." *Irrawaddy*, May 2, 2017. https://www.irrawaddy.com/news/murky-waters-burmas-law-on-pornography.html.

Jashinsky, Emily. "University Dismisses Rugby Team for Explicit Misogynistic Chant." *Campus Reform*, April 1, 2015. https://www.campusreform.org/?ID=6410.

Jeltsen, Melissa. "Trump's Budget Would Be Devastating to Poor Victims of Domestic Abuse." *Huffington Post*, March 17, 2017. https://www.huffingtonpost.com/entry/trump-budget-domestic-abuse-victims_us_58cc2184e4b0ec9d29dbd9f7.

Johnson, Megan Patricia. "Women's Access to Higher Education in Tanzania." PhD diss, Iowa University, 2011. https://ir.uiowa.edu/cgi/viewcontent.cgi?article=2618&context=etd.

Jones, Pete. "Congo: We Did Whatever We Wanted, Says Soldier Who Raped 53 Women." *Guardian*, April 11, 2013. https://www.theguardian.com/world/2013/apr/11/congo-rapes-g8-soldier.

Kakutani, Michiko. "'King Leopold's Ghost': Genocide with Spin Control." *New York Times*, Steptember 1, 1998. http://movies2.nytimes.com/books/98/08/30/daily/leopold-book-review.html.

Kant, Immanuel. *Perpetual Peace*. Edited by Lewis White Beck. New York: MacMillan, 1989.

Keller, Bill. "Apartheid's Gone, and Anything Goes." *New York Times*, December 28, 1994. https://www.nytimes.com/1994/12/28/world/apartheid-s-gone-and-anything-goes.html.

Kenyon, Bobbi-Jo. "The Effects of Televised Violence on Students." Master's thesis, Grand Valley State University, 2002.

Kertscher, Tom. "The Allegations about Donald Trump and Miss Teen USA Contestants." *Politifact*, October 18, 2016. https://www.politifact.com/wisconsin/article/2016/oct/18/allegations-about-donald-trump-and-miss-teen-usa-c/.

Khaleeli, Jehan. "Addressing the Sexual Misconduct of Peacekeepers." https://www.globalpolicy.org/component/content/article/199/40838.html.

Khan, Shaan. "What's Really Behind India's Rape Crisis." *Daily Beast*, March 25, 2016. www.thedailybeast.com/whats-really-behind-indias-rape-crisis.

Kimani, Mary. "Les femmes du Congo face aux sequelles des viols" ["Congo Women Face the Aftermath of Rape"]. *AfriqueRenouveau*, January 2007. https://www.

un.org/africarenewal/fr/magazine/january-2007/les-femmes-du-congo-face-aux-s%C3%A9quelles-des-viols.

"Kony Hunters Increasingly Disillusioned." *CBS News*, April 24, 2012. https://www.cbsnews.com/news/kony-hunters-increasingly-disillusioned/.

Koss, Mary P., and Barry R. Burkhart. "A Conceptual Analysis of Rape Victimization: Long-Term Effects and Implications for Treatment." *Psychology of Women Quarterly* 13.1 (March 1989) 27–40. https://journals.sagepub.com/doi/10.1111/j.1471-6402.1989.tb00983.x.

Kramer, Samuel Noah. *The Sumerians: Their History, Culture and Character*. Chicago: University of Chicago Press, 1963.

Kulper, Kathleen. "Olympe de Gouges." https://www.britannica.com/biography/olympe-de-gouges.

"La Justice Sud Africaine ne Veut pas de Télé Porno" ["South African Ministry of Justice Does Not Want Televised Pornography"]. *Libertarian*, January 16, 2012. https://www.liberation.fr/planete/2012/01/16/la-justice-sud-africaine-ne-veut-pas-de-tele-porno_788780.

Landay, Jonathan. "Fatwa on Who Can Rape Female Slaves." *Reuters*, December 29, 2015. https://www.reuters.com/article/us-usa-islamic-state-sexslaves-exclusive-idUS KBN0UC0AO20151230.

Lefort, Rebecca. "700 Children Born with Genetic Disabilities Due to Cousin Marriages Every Year." https://www.telegraph.co.uk/news/health/news/7957808/700-children-born-with-genetic-disabilities-due-to-cousin-marriages-every-year.html.

"Legalizing Online Porn in South Africa." https://causeforjustice.org/2018/08/28/legalising-online-pornography-in-sa/.

Legman, Gershon. *The Limerick*. New York: HarperCollins, 1976.

———. *Love and Death: A Study in Censorship*. New York: Hacker Art, 1963.

Lemsine, Aicha. "Breaking the Silence of Women's Agony in Algeria." *Washington Report on Middle East Affairs*, April/May 1995. https://www.wrmea.org/1995-april-may/breaking-the-silence-of-women-s-agony-in-algeria.html.

Liisanantti, Anu, and Karin Beese. "Gendercide: The Missing Women?" https://www.ehu.eus/documents/2007376/2226923/Gendercide.+The+missing+women.

"List of Adult Television Channels." https://en.wikipedia.org/wiki/List_of_adult_television_channels.

"List of Countries by Income Inequality." https://en.wikipedia.org/wiki/List_of_countries_by_income_equality.

"List of Ongoing Armed Conflicts." https://en.wikipedia.org/wiki/List_of_ongoing_armed_conflicts.

Lloyd-Davies, Fiona. "Why Eastern DR Congo is 'Rape Capital of the World.'" *CNN*, November 25, 2011. https://www.cnn.com/2011/11/24/world/africa/democratic-congo-rape/index.html.

MacKinnon, Catharine. *Are Women Human?* Cambridge: Belknap, 2006.

———. *Butterfly Politics*. Cambridge: Belknap, 2017.

———. "How Litigation Laid the Ground for Accountability after #MeToo." *Guardian*, December 23, 2017. https://www.theguardian.com/commentisfree/2017/dec/23/how-litigation-laid-the-ground-for-accountability-after-metoo.

———. Personal communication, February 2017–June 2018.

———. "Rape, Genocide and Women's Rights." *Harvard Women's Legal Journal* 17 (1994) 5–16.

———. *Toward a Feminist Theory of the State*. Cambridge: Harvard University Press, 1989.

———. "Turning Rape into Pornography." In *Mass Rape: The War Against Women in Bosnia-Herzegovina*, edited by Alexandra Stiglmeyer, 73–81. Lincoln: University of Nebraska Press, 1994.

MacLeod, Andrew. "The United Nations Is Turning a Blind Eye to Child Rape Within Its Own Ranks." *Independent*, March 25, 2017. https://www.independent.co.uk/voices/united-nations-soldiers-paedophilia-un-child-rape-ngo-staff-a7648791.html.

Malagardis, Maria. "L'Afrique du sud malade du viol. Avec plus d'un million de victimes par an, dont de nombreux enfants, le pays détient un triste record mondial. Et le pouvoir a décidé de réagir" ["South Africa Is Sick of Rape: With More Than a Million Victims Each Year, of Whom Many Are Children, the Country Holds a Sad World Record"]. *Liberation*, October 13, 1999. https://www.liberation.fr/planete/1999/10/13/l-afrique-du-sud-malade-du-viol-avec-plus-d-un-million-de-victimes-par-an-dont-de-nombreux-enfants-l_287783.

Marcuse, Herbert. *An Essay on Liberation*. Boston: Beacon, 1969.

"Max Waltman." https://www.statsvet.su.se/english/research/our-researchers/max-waltman-1.242621.

McPhillips, Deirdre. "The War on Women, in 5 Charts." *U.S. News*, October 20, 2016. https://www.usnews.com/news/best-countries/articles/2016-10-20/violence-against-women-in-5-charts.

McVeigh, Tracy. "Why India's 'Devadasi' Girls Face a Wretched Life in the Name of Religion." *Guardian*, January 22, 2011. https://www.theguardian.com/world/2011/jan/22/india-sex-exploitation-girls-devadasi.

Mehtal, Yagnesh. "Riots in Surat after Calf Head Found on Road." *Times of India*, January 30, 2017. https://timesofindia.indiatimes.com/city/surat/riots-in-surat-after-calf-head-found-on-road/articleshow/56871006.cms.

Melander, Erik. "The UCDP Armed Conflict Definition." http://www.undp.org/content/dam/norway/nro/images/img/sdg-16-oslo-2016/Erik%20Melander.pdf.

Meyer, Marvin, trans. *Gospel of Thomas*. San Francisco: Harper, 1992.

Miller, Cassie, and Alexandra Werner-Winslow. "Ten Days After: Harassment and Intimidation in the Aftermath of the Election." https://www.splcenter.org/20161129/ten-days-after-harassment-and-intimidation-aftermath-election.

Miller, Shari. "Pakistani Women Are Living in 'Entirely Different Society' and Are 'Shockingly Badly Integrated' in Britain Says Official Audit." *Daily Mail*, October 8, 2017. https://www.dailymail.co.uk/news/article-4960188/Pakistani-women-UK-shockingly-badly-integrated.html.

Miller, William R. et al. "The Effects of Rape on Marital and Sexual Adjustment." https://www.tandfonline.com/doi/abs/10.1080/01926188208250436.

Ministère des Armées. "Femmes dans l'armée français" ["Women in the French Army"]. https://www.defense.gouv.fr/content/download/487432/7798345/version/1/file/Les+femmes+dans+larmee+francaise-diptyque.pdf.

Monanga, Freddy. "Génocide en RDC: Honte à la Communauté Internationale" ["Genocide in the DRC: Shame on the International Community"]. *Kongo Times*, December 11, 2018. http://afrique.kongotimes.info/femmes/5936-genocide-congo-honte-capitale-mondiale-viol-mensonge-deguise-sort-laboratoires-communaute-internationale.html.

Mooney, David. "The Chilling Reality of Sexism in Football." *New Statesman America*, September 30, 2014. https://www.newstatesman.com/sport/2014/09/chilling-reality-sexism-football.

Moore, Jack. "CIA Director Mike Pompeo Says Osama Bin Laden's Porn Stash Won't Be Released." *Newsweek*, September 12, 2017. https://www.newsweek.com/cia-director-mike-pompeo-bin-laden-documents-special-forces-raid-released-663288.

Moore, Jina. "This Is What Happens to Women's Rights When the Far Right Takes Over." *Buzzfeed News*, March 11, 2017. https://www.buzzfeednews.com/article/jinamoore/polands-far-right-is-trying-to-take-away-womens-rights-and-t.

Moran, Lee. "Bill Maher Shreds GOP Official's 'Joseph and Mary' Defense of Roy Moore." *Huffington Post*, November 11, 2017. https://www.huffingtonpost.com/entry/bill-maher-roy-moore-evangelical_us_5a06a546e4b0e37d2f379665.

Morgan, Robin. "Rape, Murder, and the American GI." *Alternet*, August 16, 2006. https://www.alternet.org/story/40481/rape,_murder,_and_the_american_gi.

Moses, A. Dirk. "Raphael Lemkin, Culture, and the Concept of Genocide." In *The Oxford Handbook of Genocide Studies*, edited by Donald Bloxham and A. Dirk Moses, 19–41. Oxford: Oxford University Press, 2010. https://www.dirkmoses.com/uploads/7/3/8/2/7382125/moses_lemkin_culture.pdf.

Msuya, Norah. "Tradition and Culture in Africa: Practices that Facilitate Trafficking of Women and Children." *Dignity: A Journal on Sexual Exploitation.* 2.1 (January 2017). https://digitalcommons.uri.edu/cgi/viewcontent.cgi?article=1007&context=dignity.

Mudiaki, Priscillia. "Goma, la triste capitale du viol" ["Goma, the Sad Capital of Rape"]. https://www.opinion-internationale.com/2013/06/03/goma-la-capitale-du-viol_17939.html.

Mulumeoderhwa, M. "Forced Sex, Rape and Sexual Exploitation: Attitudes and Experiences of High School Students in South Kivu, Democratic Republic of Congo." *Cult Health Sex* 17.3 (2015) 284–95. https://www.ncbi.nlm.nih.gov/pubmed/25118073.

Mungello, D. E. *Drowning Girls in China: Female Infanticide in China Since 1650.* New York: Rowman & Littlefield, 2008.

Murphy, Heather. "What Experts Know about Men Who Rape." *New York Times*, October 30, 2017. https://www.nytimes.com/2017/10/30/health/men-rape-sexual-assault.html.

Muscati, Samer. "In Somalia, Rape is 'Normal', but the Government Can Change That." *Human Rights Watch*, March 7, 2014. https://www.hrw.org/news/2014/03/07/somalia-rape-normal-government-can-change.

Nashrullah, Tasneem. "A Militant Hindu Camp in India Is Training Young Women to Hate Themselves and Accept Their Weakness." *Buzzfeed News*, May 25, 2014. https://www.buzzfeednews.com/article/tasneemnashrulla/a-militant-hindu-camp-in-india-is-training-young-women-to-ha.

National Center for Educational Statistics. https://nces.ed.gov/fastfacts/display.asp?id=372.

National SEED Project. "White Privilege: Unpacking the Invisible Knapsack." https://nationalseedproject.org/white-privilege-unpacking-the-invisible-knapsack.

"National Sexual Violence Resource Center." https://www.nsvrc.org/.

Ncube, Leonard. "2 Pupils to Be Caned for Raping Classmate." *Chronicle*, August 27, 2016. https://www.chronicle.co.zw/2-pupils-to-be-caned-for-raping-classmate/.

Nelson, Eshe. "The UK's Conservative Government Has Put Britain's Racial Inequality on Display." *Quartz*, October 11, 2017. https://qz.com/1099723/the-uks-conservative-government-has-put-britains-racial-inequality-on-display/.

New, Jake. "Updated: Sex Assaults and Type of Institution." *Inside Higher Ed*, July 12, 2016. https://www.insidehighered.com/news/2016/07/12/study-size-type-institution-related-rates-forcible-rape.

Nolen, Stephanie. "Not Women Anymore . . . The Congo's Rape Survivors Face Pain, Shame, and AIDS." *Ms. Magazine*, 2005. http://www.msmagazine.com/spring2005/congo.asp.

Ntwari, Bernard. "UNHCR, Refugees Work Together to Prevent Rape." *UNHCR*, March 30, 2004. https://www.unhcr.org/en-us/news/latest/2004/3/40697ab57/feature-unhcr-refugees-work-together-prevent-rape.html.

Olsson, Sandra. "Congo's Girl Soldiers Struggle to Return." *New Internationalist*, June 15, 2017. https://newint.org/blog/2017/06/15/abused-and-abandoned.

Oosterhoff, Pauline. "Can Porn Be a Positive for Sex Education?" *Guardian*, December 21, 2016. https://www.theguardian.com/global-development-professionals-network/2016/dec/21/porn-positive-sex-education.

O'Reilly, Sarah, et al. "College Student Attitudes toward Pornography Use." *College Student Journal* 41.2 (June 2007) 402–6.

"Pakistan Religious Leaders Slam Women's Protection Act." *Al Jazeera*, March 3, 2016. https://www.aljazeera.com/news/2016/03/religious-leaders-slam-women-protection-act-pakistan-160303160705361.html.

Paterson, Stewart. "Mothers' Names Could FINALLY Be Included in Marriage Certificates as First Major Change to Law Since the Reign of Queen Victoria is Put Forward." *Daily Mail*, October 22, 2017. https://www.dailymail.co.uk/news/article-5005435/Marriage-certificates-FINALLY-include-mothers-names.html.

Peace Pledge Union. "Media and Violence Survey." http://archive.ppu.org.uk/chidren/media_survey1-e.html.

Pearce, Lara. "UNSW Is Investigating Following 'Appalling' Chant by Baxter College Students." *Huffington Post*, December 4, 2016. https://www.huffingtonpost.com.au/2016/04/12/baxter-college-chant_n_9668244.html.

Peoples, Steve, and Kimberly Chandler. "Moore Denies Sexual Misconduct, but GOP Fears Election Risk." *Seattle Times*, November 10, 2017. https://www.seattletimes.com/nation-world/sexual-misconduct-accusations-transform-alabama-senate-race/.

Peralta, Eyder. "U.N. Condemns 'Grotesque Rape Chants' by Burundi Youth Militia." *Goats and Soda*, April 19, 2017. https://www.npr.org/sections/goatsandsoda/2017/04/19/524703738/u-n-condemns-grotesque-rape-chants-by-burundi-youth-militia.

Picketty, Thomas. *Capital in the Twenty-First Century*. Cambridge: Harvard University Press, 2014.

Pinker, Steven. *The Better Angels of our Nature: Why Violence Has Declined*. London: Penguin, 2012.

"Playboy Enterprises." https://en.wikipedia.org/wiki/Playboy_Enterprises.

Popper, Karl. *The Logic of Scientific Discovery*. New York: Basic, 1959.

Popper-Lynkeus, Joseph. *The Individual and the Value of Human Life*. Translated by Andrew Kirk Kelley with Joram Graf Haber. Lanham: Rowman & Littlefield, 1995.

"Porn Industry, Porn Trade, Adult Entertainment Industry." *Economy Watch*, June 29, 2010. www.economywatch.com/world-industries/porn-industry.html.

"Porn in the U.S. Armed Forces: How Explicit Content May Be Influencing Military Culture." *Fight the New Drug*, April 17, 2018. https://fightthenewdrug.org/massive-porn-problem-us-military/.

"Pornography by Region." https://en.wikipedia.org/wiki/Pornography_by_region.

"PTSD: A Growing Epidemic." *NIH Medline Plus* 4.1 (Winter 2009) 10–14. https://medlineplus.gov/magazine/issues/winter09/articles/winter09pg10-14.html.

Press Trust of India. "Intl Experts Spoil Modi's Party, Say Gujarat Worse than Bosnia." *Express India*, December 19, 2002. http://archive.li/N8Nd6.

Pressly, Linda. "Resignation Syndrome: Sweden's Mystery Illness." *BBC News*, October 26, 2017. https://www.bbc.com/news/magazine-41748485.

Pretorius, Amanda. "Violence in South African Children's Television Programmes." Master's thesis, Tshwane University of Technology, 2006.

Qiu, Linda. "Emma Watson: More Lives Are Lost Due to Gender Discrimination Than in All 20th Century Wars." *Politifact*, March 15, 2016. https://www.politifact.com/global-news/statements/2016/mar/15/emma-watson/emma-watson-more-lives-are-lost-due-gender-discrim/.

RAINN. "Campus Sexual Violence: Statistics." https://www.rainn.org/statistics/campus-sexual-violence.

Rao, Naveen. "Hugh Hefner's Wiki: Cause of Death, Wife, Net Worth, Kids & 5 Facts to Know." https://www.earnthenecklace.com/hugh-hefner-wiki-cause-of-death-wife-net-worth-kids-facts/.

"Rape, Abuse and Incest National Network." https://www.rainn.org/.

"Rape in India." https://en.wikipedia.org/wiki/Rape_in_India.

"Rape Statistics." https://en.wikipedia.org/wiki/Rape_statistics.

"Rapport sur le génocide au Cong: Kigali refuse de mourir seul" ["Report on the Genocide in Congo: Kigali Refuses to Die Alone"]. *le Phare*, September 1, 2010. http://new.lephareonline.net/rapport-sur-le-genocide-au-congo-kigali-refuse-de-mourir-seul/.

Rashtrya Swayamsevak Sangh (RSS) Training Camp. https://thewire.in/184044.

Rasmussen, Sune Engel, and Haroon Janjua. "Pakistani Police Arrest Men for Marching Girl Naked through Village." *Guardian*, November 2, 2017. https://www.theguardian.com/world/2017/nov/02/pakistani-police-arrest-men-for-marching-girl-naked-through-village.

Ras-Work, Berhane. "The Impact of Harmful Traditional Practices on the Girl Child." http://www.un.org/womenwatch/daw/egm/elim-disc-viol-girlchild/ExpertPapers/EP.4%20%20%20Raswork.pdf.

"RDC: Le Rapport final de l'ONU atteste de l'agression du pays par le Rwanda" ["DRC: Final UN Report Attests to Aggression against DRC by Rwanda"]. *Kongo Times*, November 16, 2012. http://afrique.kongotimes.info/rdc/politique/5215-agression-rapport-onu-sanctions-rwanda-m23-fermeture-frontiere-congo-ouganda-bunagana.html.

Reisman, Judith. "A Few Brief Cites on Pornography as Contributing to the Violence against Children and Women—Including Serial Rape Murder." http://www.drjudithreisman.com/archives/Pornography%20and%20Rape%20Murder.pdf.

Religion Today. "Burmese Troops Gang-Rape Woman in Church." *Christian Headlines*, n.d. https://www.christianheadlines.com/blog/burmese-troops-gang-rape-woman-in-church.html.

Replogle, Elaine. Personal communication, October 2017.

———. "The Psychology of Gang Rape." *Role Reboot*, January 16, 2013. http://www.rolereboot.org/culture-and-politics/details/2013-01-the-psychology-of-gang-rape.

Reynolds, George M., and Amanda Shendruk. "Demographics of the U.S. Military." https://www.cfr.org/article/demographics-us-military.

RFI. "Afrique du Sud: homage après le viol collectif et le meurtre d'une jeune fille" ["South Africa: Tribute after the Gang Rape and Murder of a Young Girl"]. *Afrique*, October 2, 2013. http://www.rfi.fr/afrique/20130210-afrique-sud-hommage-apres-le-viol-collectif-le-meurtre-une-jeune-fille-Anene-Booysen.

Richmond, Ray. "Playboy Snaps Up Rival Spice." *Variety*, February 4, 1998. https://variety.com/1998/tv/news/playboy-snaps-up-rival-spice-1117467419/.

"रणरागिणी शाखेच्या वतीने नवरात्रोत्सवानिमित्त केलेल्या प्रबोधनाचा ३०० हून अधिक भाविक महिलांकडून लाभ!" ["More Than 300 Devotees Benefitted from the Festival for Awareness of Navratri on Behalf of the Ranaragini Branch!"]. *Hindu Jagruti*, October 13, 2016. https://www.hindujagruti.org/marathi/news/16566.html.

"Rome Statute of the International Criminal Court." https://www.icc-cpi.int/resourcelibrary/official-journal/rome-statute.aspx.

Russell, Diana. "US Pornography Invades South Africa." In *Radically Speaking: Feminism Reclaimed*, edited by Diane Bell and Renate Klein, 429–35. Melbourne: Spinifex, 1996.

Russon, Gabrielle. "Panel Finds Frat Cited for UCF Rape-Chant Broke No Rules." *Orlando Sentinel*, December 12, 2018. https://www.orlandosentinel.com/features/education/84252901-132.html.

Sahani, Alaka. "What Salman Said Was Unfortunate and Insensitive: Aamir Khan." *Indian Express*, July 6, 2016. https://indianexpress.com/article/entertainment/bollywood/salman-khan-aamir-khan-sultan-dangal-rape-remark-unfortunate-and-insensitive-2893935/.

Sallin, Karl, et al. "Resignation Syndrome: Catatonia? Culture Bound?" *Frontiers in Behavioral Neuroscience* 10.7 (2016). https://www.ncbi.nlm.nih.gov/pmc/articles/PMC4731541/.

Saner, Emine. "Women and Men Are Speaking Out about Abuse—Is This the End of the Patriarchy?" *Guardian*, October 31, 2017. https://www.theguardian.com/lifeandstyle/2017/oct/30/speaking-out-abuse-end-patriarchy-weinstein-allegations-sexual-abuse.

Sanyai, Anindita. "After UP's 'Anti-Romeo Squad,' Haryana Launches 'Operation Durga.'" *NDTV*, April 13, 2017. https://www.ndtv.com/india-news/after-ups-anti-romeo-squad-haryana-launches-operation-durga-to-ensure-womens-safety-1680738.

SAPA. "'Sunday Rapist' Admits Porn, Child Porn Addiction." *Times Live*, August 28, 2012. https://www.timeslive.co.za/news/south-africa/2012-08-28-sunday-rapist-admits-porn-child-porn-addiction/.

Sawyer, Kem Knapp, and John Sawyer. "Congo's Children." https://pulitzercenter.atavist.com/webcongoschildren.

Scaruffi, Pietro. "Wars and Casualties of the 20th and 21st Centuries." https://www.scaruffi.com/politics/massacre.html.

Schlein, Lisa. "UN: Huge Surge in DRC Refugees Fleeing to Zambia." *VOA News*, October 3, 2017. https://www.voanews.com/a/drc-refugees-fleeing-to-zambia/4054346.html.

Schweitzer, Albert. *Quest for the Historical Jesus*. New York: MacMillan, 1966.

Searcey, Dionne. "They Fled Boko Haram Only to Be Raped by Nigerian Security Forces." *New York Times,* December 8, 2017. https://www.nytimes.com/2017/12/08/world/africa/boko-haram-nigeria-security-forces-rape.html.

"Selon Google, six pays les plus adeptes de sites pornographiques sur huit sont musulmans" ["According to Google, Six of the Eight Nations with the Most Pornography Sites Are Muslim"]. *Europe-Israel News*, May 20, 2015. https://www.europe-israel.

org/2015/05/selon-google-six-pays-les-plus-adeptes-de-sites-pornographiques-sont-musulmans/.

Sen, Amartya. "More Than 100 Million Women Are Missing." *New York Review of Books*, December 20, 1990. https://www.nybooks.com/articles/1990/12/20/more-than-100-million-women-are-missing/.

Sequeira, D., et al. "The Kingdom Has Not Yet Come: Coping with Microinequities within a Christian University." *Research on Christian Higher Education* 2 (1995) 1–35.

Sexual and Gender Based Violence against Refugees, Returnees, and Internally Placed Persons. N.p.: United Nations High Commission for Refugees, 2003. https://www.unicef.org/emerg/files/gl_sgbv03.pdf.

"Sigma Chi Chants." http://www.greekchat.com/gcforums/showthread.php?t=81422.

Singh, Kanishka. "Sexism and Misogyny Must Come to an End in Indian Politics." *Indian Express*, December 11, 2018. https://indianexpress.com/article/opinion/web-edits/sexism-and-misogyny-must-come-to-an-end-in-indian-politics-4490945/.

"Shamhat." https://en.wikipedia.org/wiki/Shamhat.

Shengold, Leonard. *Soul Murder: The Effects of Childhood Abuse and Deprivation.* New York: Ballantine, 1991.

———. "Soul Murder Revisited: Thoughts about Therapy, Hate, Love, and Memory." *New York Times*, 1999. http://movies2.nytimes.com/books/first/s/shengold-soul.html.

Shields, Nancy, and Jeremy Kane. "Social and Psychological Correlates of Internet Use among College Students." *Cyberpsychology* 5.1 (2011).

Shingal, Ankur. "The Devadasi System: Temple Prostitution in India." *UCLA Women's Law Journal* 22.1 (2015). https://cloudfront.escholarship.org/dist/prd/content/qt37z853br/qt37z853br.pdf.

Sigsworth, Romi. "'Anyone Can Be a Rapist': An Overview of Sexual Violence in South Africa." Johannesburg: Centre for the Study of Violence and Reconciliation, 2009. https://www.researchgate.net/profile/Romi_Sigsworth/publication/242680413_Centre_for_the_Study_of_Violence_and_Reconciliation_CSVR/links/00b7d534961c16644d000000/Centre-for-the-Study-of-Violence-and-Reconciliation-CSVR.pdf.

Solis, Marie. "Alabama State Rep. Says Roy Moore's Accusers Should Be Prosecuted." *Newsweek*, November 10, 2017. https://www.newsweek.com/alabama-state-rep-says-roy-moores-accusers-should-be-prosecuted-708125.

Solnit, Rebecca. "A Rape a Minute, a Thousand Corpses a Year." *Nation*, January 24, 2013. https://www.thenation.com/article/rape-minute-thousand-corpses-year/.

Solomon, Salem, and Bagassi Koura. "Gang Rapes in Mali Prompt Anger, Calls for Reform." *Voice of America*, February 18, 2018. https://www.voanews.com/a/gang-rapes-mali-anger-calls-for-reform/4259582.html.

Sommers, Christina Hoff. "The War Against Boys." *Atlantic*, May 2000. https://www.theatlantic.com/magazine/archive/2000/05/the-war-against-boys/304659/.

"South Africa; More and More Women Killed." *BBC News Afrique*, May 24, 2017. https://www.bbc.com/afrique/region-40036469.

"Special Adviser of the Secretary-General on the Prevention of Genocide." http://www.un.org/en/genocideprevention/special-adviser-prevention-genocide.html.

Stack, Liam. "Light Sentence for Brock Turner in Stanford Rape Case Draws Outrage." *New York Times*, June 6, 2016. https://www.nytimes.com/2016/06/07/us/outrage-in-stanford-rape-case-over-dueling-statements-of-victim-and-attackers-father.html.

Stanton, Gregory. "The 8 Stages of Genocide." http://www.genocidewatch.org/genocide/8stagesofgenocide.html.

―――. "Countries at Risk Report—2012." http://www.genocidewatch.org/images/Countries_at_Risk_Report_2012.pdf.

St. Clair, Stacy, and Gregory Pratt. "Northwestern University Investigates Reports of Sex Assaults, Drugging at Frats." *Chicago Tribune*, December 12, 2018. https://www.chicagotribune.com/news/local/breaking/ct-northwestern-date-rape-alert-fraternity-20170207-story.html.

Stewart, Heather, and Rowena Mason. "Michael Fallon Quits as Defence Secretary, Saying His Behaviour Has 'Fallen Short.'" *Guardian*, November 1, 2017. https://www.theguardian.com/politics/2017/nov/01/michael-fallon-quits-as-defence-secretary.

Stuart, Tessa. "A Timeline of Donald Trump's Creepiness While He Owned Miss Universe." *Rolling Stone,* October 12, 2016. https://www.rollingstone.com/politics/politics-features/a-timeline-of-donald-trumps-creepiness-while-he-owned-miss-universe-191860/.

Summers, Hannah. "Fighting Child Sex Crimes in South Africa: 'We've Seen an Increase in Brutality.'" *Guardian*, December 21, 2017. https://www.theguardian.com/global-development/2017/dec/21/fighting-child-sex-crimes-south-africa-support-clinic.

Sweetman, Caroline, ed. *Violence Against Women.* London: Oxfam, 1998.

Swinford, Steven. "First Cousin Marriages in Pakistani Communities Leading to 'Appalling' Disabilities among Children." *Telegraph*, July 7, 2015. https://www.telegraph.co.uk/news/health/children/11723308/First-cousin-marriages-in-Pakistani-communities-leading-to-appalling-disabilities-among-children.html.

Szymanski, Dawn M., et al. "Sexual Objectification of Women: Advances to Theory and Research." *The Counseling Psychologist* 39 (2011) 6–38.

"Take a Test—Project Implicit." https://implicit.harvard.edu/implicit/takeatest.html.

"Timeline of Women's Suffrage." https://en.wikipedia.org/wiki/Timeline_of_women%27s_suffrage.

Thomas Reuters Foundation. https://news.trust.org/womens-rights/.

Thomas, Sandra P. "Resignation Syndrome: Is It a New Phenomenon or Is It Catatonia?" *Issues in Mental Health Nursing* 38.7 (2017) 531–32.

Thompson, Lisa L. "The Global Supply Chain of Sexual Exploitation and the Necessity of Combating the Demand for Commercial Sex." *Dignity* 2.3 (2017).

Timmons, Heather. "Why Do Groups of Men Attack Lone Women?" *New York Times*, December 20, 2012. https://india.blogs.nytimes.com/2012/12/20/understanding-the-psychology-of-gang-rape/.

Townsend, Mark. "Women and Children 'Endure Rape, Beatings and Abuse' inside Dunkirk's Refugee Camp." *Guardian*, February 11, 2017. https://www.theguardian.com/world/2017/feb/12/dunkirk-child-refugees-risk-sexual-violence.

"Transcript: Donald Trump's Taped Comments about Women." https://www.nytimes.com/2016/10/08/us/donald-trump-tape-transcript.html.

Trzyna, Thomas. *Blessed Are the Pacifists: The Beatitudes and Just War Theory.* Harrisonburg, VA: Herald, 2006.

―――. *Cain's Crime: The Proliferation of Weapons and the Targeting of Civilians in Contemporary War.* Eugene, OR: Cascade, 2018.

―――. *Karl Popper and Literary Theory: Critical Rationalism as a Philosophy of Literature.* Series in the Philosophy of Karl R. Popper and Critical Rationalism 22. Leiden: Brill, 2017.

———. *Meeting God*. Asuncion, Paraguay: University Press of the South, 2009.

Tuohy, Wendy. "Rougher, Harder, Violent: How Porn Is Warping the Male Mind." *Daily Telegraph*, July 23, 2015. https://www.dailytelegraph.com.au/rendezview/rougher-harder-violent-how-porn-is-warping-the-male-mind/news-story/504698ce318f551052847f13ac678fd1.

"Une télé-réalité porno débarque en Afrique du sud" ["A Pornographic Reality Show Starts in South Africa"]. *Seneweb*, March 31, 2011. http://www.seneweb.com/news/Afrique/une-tele-realite-porno-debarque-en-afrique-du-sud_n_43176.html.

UN Family Rights Caucus. "The Porn Pandemic." http://unfamilyrightscaucus.org/family-policy-resources/documentaries/the-porn-pandemic/.

UNICEF. "Maternal Mortality." https://data.unicef.org/topic/maternal-health/maternal-mortality/.

United Nations. "Annual Review 2016." https://undocs.org/A/71/2.

———. "Annual Review 2003." https://undocs.org/A/58/2(SUPP).

United Nations Special Rapporteur on the Sale of Children, Child Prostitution and Child Pornography. "25 Years of Fighting the Sale and Sexual Exploitation of Children: Addressing New Challenges." https://www.ohchr.org/Documents/Issues/Children/SR/25YearsMandate.pdf.

United Nations Statistics Division. "The World's Women 2015." https://unstats.un.org/unsd/gender/worldswomen.html.

United Nations Treaty Collection. "Optional Protocol for the Convention on the Rights of the Child." https://treaties.un.org/pages/viewdetails.aspx?src=ind&mtdsg_no=iv-11-b&chapter=4&lang=en.

"United Nations Office on Drugs and Crime." https://www.unodc.org/unodc/en/data-and-analysis/statistics/index.html.

"United Nations Office on Genocide Prevention and the Responsibility to Protect." http://www.un.org/en/genocideprevention/genocide.html.

United States Department of Labor. "Findings on the Worst Forms of Child Labor." https://www.dol.gov/agencies/ilab/resources/reports/child-labor/findings.

"United States Military Casualties of War." https://en.wikipedia.org/wiki/United_States_military_casualties_of_war.

"Universal Declaration of Human Rights." www.un.org/en/universal-declaration-human-rights.

"U.S. Forest Products Industry—Statistics & Facts." https://www.statista.com/topics/1316/forest-products-industry/.

"U.S. Military World War 2." https://www.nationalww2museum.org/.

"US Pushing for Resolution to Sex Abuse Cases Involving UN Peacekeepers." *Guardian*, March 4, 2016. https://www.theguardian.com/world/2016/mar/04/un-peacekeepers-sex-abuse-allegations-us-resolution.

Vagianos, Alanna. "Gretchen Carlson on Harvey Weinstein Allegations: 'This Is the Watershed Moment.'" *Huffington Post*, October 17, 2017. https://www.huffingtonpost.com/entry/gretchen-carlson-on-harvey-weinstein-allegations-this-is-the-watershed-moment_us_59e6090fe4b02a215b334316.

Venugopal, Vasudha. "What Does It Take to Be an RSS Karyakarta?" *Economic Times*, May 30, 2018. https://economictimes.indiatimes.com/news/politics-and-nation/what-does-it-take-to-be-an-rss-karyakarta/articleshow/64390472.cms.

Viktor Bout. https://en.wikipedia.org/wiki/Viktor_Bout.

Vincent, Coralie. "Oscar Pistorius aurait regardé du porno avant de tirer sur Reeva Steenkamp" ["Oscar Pistorius Watched Pornography before Shooting Reeva Steenkamp"]. *Closer*, February 24, 2014. https://www.closermag.fr/vecu/faits-divers/oscar-pistorius-aurait-regarde-du-porno-avant-de-tirer-sur-reeva-steenkamp-279919.

Vincent, Peter. "Australian MP Gives Harrowing Speech about Finding Husband's Child Pornography." *Telegraph*, September 7, 2017. https://www.telegraph.co.uk/news/2017/09/07/australian-mp-gives-harrowing-speech-finding-husbands-child/.

"Violence in the Media: Psychologists Study Potential Harmful Effects." www.apa.org/action/resources/research-in-action/protect.aspx.

"Viol et meurtre d'une religieuse en Afrique du Sud: trois hommes arêtés" ["Rape and murder of a nun in South Africa: three men arrested"]. *BFMTV*, April 28, 2015. https://www.bfmtv.com/international/viol-et-meurtre-d-une-religieuse-en-afrique-du-sud-trois-hommes-arretes-881772.html.

Vishva Hindu Parishad. "Durga Vahini." http://vhp.org/VHP-glance/youth/durga-vahini/.

Wade, Carole, and Carol Tavris. "The Longest War: Gender and Culture." In *The Longest War: Sex Differences in Perspective*, 121–26. San Diego: Haracourt, 1984.

Ward, Mark. "Web Porn: Just How Much is There?" *BBC News*, July 1, 2013. https://www.bbc.com/news/technology-23030090.

"Women in Pakistan." https://en.wikipedia.org/wiki/Women_in_Pakistan.

"Women in the Military by Country." https://en.wikipedia.org/wiki/Women_in_the_military_by_country.

"Women in the United States Army." https://en.wikipedia.org/wiki/Women_in_the_United_States_Army.

"Women's Protection Bill." https://en.wikipedia.org/wiki/Women%27s_Protection_Bill.

Wordwatch. "The Female of the Species." https://wordwatchtowers.wordpress.com/2010/05/07/the-female-of-the-species/.

World Economic Forum. "The Global Gender Gap Report 2016." http://reports.weforum.org/global-gender-gap-report-2016/.

"World Happiness Report 2017." http://worldhappiness.report/ed/2017/.

Yasmin, Seema. "The Ebola Rape Epidemic No One's Talking About." *Foreign Policy*, February 2, 2016. https://foreignpolicy.com/2016/02/02/the-ebola-rape-epidemic-west-africa-teenage-pregnancy/.

Young-Powell, Abby. "First-Year Students 'Encouraged to Sing Necrophiliac Chant' by Union Reps." *Guardian*, October 8, 2014. https://www.theguardian.com/education/2014/oct/08/freshers-students-sing-necrophiliac-sexist-violent-chant.

Zengerle, Patricia. "For Women at the U.S. Congress: The Right to Bare Arms?" *Reuters*, July 13, 2017. https://www.reuters.com/article/us-usa-congress-dresscode-idUSKBN19Y2BV.

Zuma, Jacob. "Address by President Jacob Zuma during the launch of the National Dialogues on Violence against Women and Children." https://www.gov.za/speeches/president-jacob-zuma-launch-national-dialogues-violence-against-women-and-children-25-nov.